What's Your Sexual IQ?

What's Your Sexual IQ?

EVE MARX

CITADEL PRESS
Kensington Publishing Corp.
www.kensingtonbooks.com

CITADEL PRESS BOOKS are published by

Kensington Publishing Corp.
850 Third Avenue
New York, NY 10022

All Kensington titles, imprints, and distributed lines are available at special quantity discounts for bulk purchases for sales promotions, premiums, fund-raising, educational, or institutional use. Special book excerpts or customized printings can also be created to fit specific needs. For details, write or phone the office of the Kensington special sales manager: Kensington Publishing Corp., 850 Third Avenue, New York, NY 10022, attn: Special Sales Department; phone 1-800-221-2647.

CITADEL PRESS and the Citadel logo are Reg. U.S. Pat. & TM Off.

First printing: August 2004

10 9 8 7 6 5 4 3 2 1

Printed in the United States of America

Library of Congress Control Number: 2004106002

ISBN 0-8065-2610-6

Contents

Acknowledgments   vii

Introduction   ix

The Birds and The Bees   1

Masturbation and Orgasm   21

Aphrodisiacs   31

Lubes and Toys   45

Oral Sex   53

Positions   59

Anal Sex   69

It's All How You Say It: Sexual Slang   79

Sexual Health   93

Threesomes, Orgies, Gangbangs, and Gender-Benders   121

Strange Sexual Ephemera   129

Modern Technological Breakthroughs   145

That's Entertainment! Sex in the Culture   151

Sex and the Law   173

Sexual Personalities   185

The *Kama Sutra*   205

Interpreting Your Ultimate Score   217

References   219

About the Author   221

Acknowledgments

I'D LIKE TO THANK my hardworking agent, June Clark, and my wonderful and generous editor, Bob Shuman for helping to make this book happen. June and Bob, in my book, you are both tops. For the actual writing of this book, I thank my many friends who volunteered to take portions of the quiz as I was writing it, as well as my extremely forthcoming and bold pals who offered to share with me their most intimate sex histories, sexual preferences, and, sometimes, to my alarm, their most shocking sexual exploits. I apologize if I put my hands over my ears; despite all evidence to the contrary, I am a bit of a prude. I'd also like to thank my family who clued me in on fresh slang, pointed out sexy bits to me in music lyrics and movies, and who let me plow through their bathroom stashes of *Revolver* and *Maxim* magazines. I also want very much to thank my husband, who, after all these years, still loves having sex with me.

Introduction

MY LONG ROAD to becoming a "sexpert," that is, an expert on sex, is a saga. The path and direction my life took was, as one might well imagine, neither straight nor very straight-laced. Acquiring an exceptionally high sexual "IQ"—that is, a deep and varied understanding of sex—was a lesson that took years. I never set out to be a person highly knowledgeable about sex: I confess that during my twenties, my only sexual goal was to enhance my own performance and see how many partners I could wow with everything I'd learned. Understanding exactly how things work or collecting data of somewhat prurient interest certainly never crossed my mind, at least not on a conscious level. It was only much, much later that I realized my natural curiosity about sex would become an influence and, to some degree, guide almost all my life choices for as long as I consider myself to be an alive, sexual being.

Obviously, not everyone who has an interest and curiosity about sex turns out to be a sex expert. Looking back through the years, I can now see early on, there were signs hinting at the direction of my interest. I was eight years old when I started reading my cousin's *Playboys*, and I do mean really reading them, absorbing all the information the magazine had to offer, cover to cover, month after month. Later, in my early teens, I began sampling my uncle's bookshelves for more advanced literature. Among his weighty tomes were the works of Havelock Ellis, including *My Life*, *Sexual Inversion*, and *Man and Woman*, which is where I learned the meaning of cunnilingus and fellatio. Through my uncle's well stocked and wonderfully uncensored personal library, I also discovered John Cleland, who wrote *Memoirs of a Woman of Pleasure*, published in 1748 and believed to be the most famous erotic novel in the English language. I devoured the very saucy *Couples*, a novel about suburban swapping in the '60s by John Updike, as well as two spicy books, *Tropic of Cancer*, and *Sexus*, by Henry Miller, the famous writer and friend to erotic diarist Anaïs Nin. I scoured the writings of the great anthropologist Margaret Mead for the juicy parts of her *Coming of Age in Samoa*, a virtual field guide to the cultural practices of native Polynesians. Sometimes my reading choices got me in hot water with teachers, but I didn't want to stop reading racy books. So I developed ways to write and talk about what I was reading without setting off any alarms. The trick, I figured out, was never to use any so-called "dirty words," unless they were bracketed in quotation marks.

I DECIDED to write *What's Your Sexual IQ?* because I'm always interested in how sex works. I like observing how knowledge about sex can enhance overall life experiences. That's why I love keeping abreast of sex trivia, sex in the news, and the newest technological advances. I'd rather read a sexy book than a nonsexy one. In fact, I'd rather write a sexy book than a non-sexy one!

Other than increasing your own carnal thrills, you might be wondering what else having so much sexual knowledge can do for you. Sexual knowledge isn't just about new positions or tricks. Your continued well-being and health, for example, are excellent reasons to know as much as you can about sex. Under-standing of reproduction and birth control helps prevent unwanted pregnancies. Understanding how sexually transmitted diseases are passed from one person to another may save you from an annoying case of crabs, or spare you from HIV.

A seemingly unimportant but in fact excellent reason to have a high sexual IQ is that it almost guarantees you'll be the life of any party. A person who is sexually knowledgeable has something to contribute to almost any conversation, any discourse, in nearly any social circle and on any topic, including politics, history, music, film, and art.

I also wrote this book for sexually curious people because I know if I'm very interested in something, chances are, so are other people! *What's Your Sexual IQ?* is set up in a question-and-answer format. The questions are quite a challenge, but I made them that way on purpose! They begin with basic physiological questions about sex, and move on to erogenous zones and masturbation and orgasm. From there we progress to the great world of aphrodisiacs, lubricants, and sex toys. Oral sex, positions, and anal sex are the next level of challenge, followed by questions on sexual slang. The important topic of sexual health includes questions on basic contraception. More esoteric and complicated questions on threesomes, gender-benders, and other group sex questions come next. Strange sexual ephemera (what might be called trivia) is the next section, followed by modern technological breakthroughs and questions about sex in popular culture. Legal issues surrounding sex, including famous obscenity cases, is next, followed by questions on intriguing sexual personalities. The final section asks questions based on knowledge of the *Kama Sutra*, an amazing and fascinating reference book that has been called the great East Indian "bible" of sex.

It's only natural that people looking at this book will want to know, "What does it mean to have a high sexual IQ? Will a high score prove I am a superior lover?" The answer, in a way, is yes. It should go without saying that the more you know about sex, the better your odds at being skillful at it. But the real reason why you should want to determine, and hopefully improve your sexual IQ is because it will help you become a better person. A more knowledgeable person. A more enlightened and aware person. And, ultimately, a more interesting person.

What's Your Sexual IQ? is meant to test your existing knowledge about sexuality, although not necessarily your pre-test sexual performance. You are meant to have fun with the book! Scoring is simple. You score ten points for every question correctly answered. At the end of the book is a final tally which will reveal to you and your fellow players whether you are a "Libidiot" or a "Sexpert" or something in between. At the end of the day, it probably doesn't matter how you score . . . as long as you have a great time doing it.

What's Your
Sexual IQ?

The Birds
and the Bees

Remember when you were rather young and the entire topic of sex was coyly referred to as "the birds and the bees," a kind of verbal shorthand for the strange and magical processes of attraction, mating, and reproduction? The quaint-sounding phrase, incidentally, originated during the latter part of the 1800s as a euphemism for sex education. The great songwriter Cole Porter alluded to "the birds and the bees" in his 1928 tune "Let's Do It (Let's Fall in Love)," noting that birds, bees, "even educated fleas" fall in love.

This portion of the quiz focuses on three primary aspects, namely, body parts, arousal and erogenous zones, and measurements. Body parts obviously refers to both male and female genitalia, and other delectable, possibly not so wet or turgid portions of the body. Arousal and erogenous zones deals with becoming excited as well as places on the body where buttons get pushed. The last portion of this section is about the all-important business of size and measurement. You probably already know some of this information, so get ready to test your knowledge!

Body Parts

Eyes, ears, lips, noses, necks, shoulders, midriffs, thighs, calves, breasts and buttocks and feet. When you start thinking about the human body, what often leaps to mind are all the bits and pieces. In fact, in England they call their body parts "bits," and when they say "that bit looks a bit rough," they are offering a rueful allusion to a bit that is not up to snuff. This portion of the quiz is meant to test your knowledge on the proper terminology and usage of the portions of the anatomy affiliated with sex and sexual pleasure.

1. In both Latin and medical jargon, that enticing pad of fat that covers the female pubic bone is called:
   a. Mons pubis
   b. Pudenda
   c. Mons veneris
   d. Vulva

2. TRUE OR FALSE. Generally speaking, men's nipples are far more sensitive than women's nipples.

3. Physically, we've got more in common with the apes than we like to think. Which major erogenous zone reveals our sexual connection to primates?
   a. The breasts
   b. The neck
   c. The area behind the knees
   d. The buttocks

4. It's been said that the penis is the original sex toy. Apart from the usual mouth games one can play with the penis, what are the other primary playful events?
   a. You can stroke it
   b. You can fondle it
   c. You can cause it to ejaculate
   d. All of the above

5. Masturbating oneself or one's male partner right to the brink of orgasm one hour before actual lovemaking will produce what result?
   a. Prostate secretion will be increased.
   b. Delaying orgasm will result in more intense feelings during the orgasmic moments.
   c. The man's erection during lovemaking will be firmer and harder and longer lasting.
   d. Blue balls.

6. The biological purpose of the scrotum is to:
   a. Hold the balls in their proper place
   b. Keep the balls or testes at the correct temperature for optimum sperm production
   c. Protect the balls from injury
   d. To enhance the appearance of the testes

7. Native and aboriginal couples in undeveloped pockets around the world have been known to practice a select version of intercourse using this often neglected orifice:
   a. The ear
   b. The nostrils
   c. The navel
   d. The anus

8. Which often-overlooked body part is also an erotic instrument that can be used for stimulating both the clitoris and the vulva?
   a. The big toe
   b. The nose
   c. The pinky
   d. The elbow

9. Another term for the part of the anatomy known as the glans penis is:
   a. Frenulum
   b. Balanus
   c. Meatus
   d. Smegma

10. The prepuce is what part of the penis?
    a. The piece cut away during infant circumcision
    b. The free fold of skin that more or less covers the head of the glans penis
    c. The foreskin
    d. All of the above

11. Many people have pondered the relationship between the length of a woman's labia and her ability to fully enjoy sex. What is that relationship?
    a. The length of a woman's labia has no effect and makes no difference at all in terms of her sexual response.
    b. The longer the labia, the more intense the woman's orgasm.
    c. Longer labia indicate that it's going to take a longer amount of time for this woman to become aroused.
    d. It makes no difference, as all labia are more or less the same size.

Answers to Body Parts

1. c. The mons veneris is also known as the "Mound of Venus" or "Mountain of Love." The medical terminology comes from the Latin, where veneris refers to Venus, the name given by

the Romans to their goddess of love. The "mountain" is an allusion to the puffy appearance of a robust mons, an area covered by fatty tissue. At the onset of puberty, when estrogen levels increase, a distinctive mound is formed, frequently visible through tight or wet clothing. This fatty tissue, from a physiological point of view, is believed to provide a plump protective cushion between the woman's pubic bone and her partner during the act of intercourse.

2. True. Men's nipples tend to be more sensitive than those of a woman, possibly because Mother Nature intended female nipples to be sucked on, and not just by lovers. Ask any nursing mom about a teething baby and you'll understand why female nipples are designed to handle a good chewing. Although male nipples are more delicate and tender, it's a rare man who can have an orgasm just because someone is sucking on them. Many women (yes, even nursing mothers!), however, can come to orgasm that way.

3. d. If you said "buttocks," your guess is correct. Human sexual fascination with the posterior can be traced back to our origins and connection to the apes. Chimpanzees, for example, have very brightly colored buttocks. One early example of our fascination with the buttocks, or gluteus maximus, can be seen in the sculpture fetishes of the Mousterian people, a Stone Age culture that produced large-buttocked figurines, which may be seen as fertility symbols or an early version of pornography, depending on your anthropological viewpoint.

4. d. Stroking and fondling to the point of orgasm are playful activities two or more people can do with a penis.

5. a. Masturbating—but not ejaculating—an hour before intercourse will build up the prostate secretion (i.e., ejaculate), making for a more intense, forceful, bigger spurt when the big moment arrives. This masturbating/holding-off technique has been used by Hindu yogis for centuries. Some sex therapists also advise it as a technique for helping premature ejaculators to learn how to delay their orgasm.

6. b. The biological purpose of the scrotum is purely reproductive. Testes temperatures should ideally be two degrees below abdominal temperature to reap the most out of the sperm function. That's why nature provided the sac. One's sexual partner may find the scrotum fascinating and want to play with it. In bed, the rule on this should be: *ask permission first.*

7. c. While it is a dead end, the navel is wired for sensation and is perfectly capable of admitting a finger, tongue, the tip of a penis, or even a big toe. Especially a big toe. Believe it or not, if the person has enough meat on them, you can have sex with someone's bellybutton as long as they hold up the skin on either side of their navel in an imitation of labia.

8. a. The big toe, particularly the male big toe, is a built-in sex toy that Asian and East Indian lovers have enjoyed for years. For some reason, North Americans just don't give the same consideration to their feet. The pad of the male big toe, in fact, may be used quite successfully to stroke and stimulate the clitoris, even in risky public settings, such as under the table in a busy restaurant. The main thing for the toe user to remember is to be gentle, be slow, and always keep the toenail clipped short and smoothly filed. Even in an extremely public situation it is possible to give maximum sexual pleasure to your partner using only your big toe, and no one will be the wiser.

9. b. Balanus may sound like a species of whale, but it is a synonym for glans penis, which is the head or crown of the penis, and is made up of highly sensitive tissue. The frenulum is the Y-shaped web of skin connecting the foreskin to the underside of the head of the penis. The meatus is the opening at the tip of the penis that allows the passage of semen and urine. Smegma is a substance with the texture of cheese that is secreted by the glands on each side of the frenulum in uncircumcised men.

10. d. The prepuce is the retractable covering of skin that partially or completely sheathes the glans of an uncircumcised male. Actually, there is a female prepuce that covers the tip of the clitoris and retracts when the female is sufficiently aroused, but we're focusing on male prepuces here. During an infant circumcision, this bit of loose skin is partially or totally removed. Some say that's a pity, as the prepuce is simply wild with sensitive tissue. There are postings on Internet forums discussing how a man can create for himself a new foreskin, involving seemingly painful skin-stretching techniques, but short of plastic surgery, no realistic solutions have been given.

11. a. The findings of the sex researchers Masters and Johnson showed that no known relationship exists between the length (or, for that matter, thickness) of a woman's labia and her ability to enjoy sex, or the depth of her sexual response. Some women with short, thin labial lips can have mind-blowing orgasms, while some women with plump, longer, wide ones may benefit from long sessions of foreplay to achieve any orgasm and vice-versa.

Arousal and Erogenous Zones

We all know where we like to be touched. Some people only respond to traditional erogenous zones, like the genitalia, while others yearn to be touched elsewhere, like behind the knee or their armpits! You may be surprised at some of the material covered in this section—and you might try it for yourself or with a partner!

1. What is the most sensitive sex organ on a human being?
   a. The penis
   b. The vulva
   c. The brain
   d. The skin

2. Which of the following is a major erogenous zone for women but not for men?
   a. Vagus
   b. Carotid artery
   c. Jugular
   d. Clavicle

3. What common human activity not usually associated with sex might induce, in some people, glorious orgasm?
   a. Scratching
   b. Tickling
   c. Washing
   d. Spitting

4. What is the original meaning of the term "shampoo"? To:
   a. Gently massage and knead someone all over
   b. Wash the hair
   c. Cleanse and specifically take care of the feet
   d. Ejaculate

5. The best way to moisten an erogenous area in preparation for lovemaking is to do what to it?
   a. Use a love lube or love gel
   b. Take a damp washcloth to it
   c. Give it a good drubbing with a Wet One
   d. Lick it

6. If you're licking and breathing into someone's ear, what must you do to avoid deafening your partner?
   a. Breathe in, not out
   b. Breathe out, not in
   c. Don't breathe too loudly
   d. Don't breathe at all

7. Love bites, sometimes crudely known as hickeys, are created by doing what to the skin?
   a. Nipping it
   b. Chewing it
   c. Biting it
   d. Kissing it with a strong suction action

8. What exactly is the G-Spot?
   a. The G-Spot is the female prostate gland.
   b. The G-Spot is an erogenous zone within the vagina made up of specialized glands and ducts.
   c. The G-Spot is a second clitoris.
   d. The G-Spot is an urban legend and no such thing exists except in an old porno movie.

9. Some women can experience orgasm from having their mons veneris stroked or massaged. A woman's ability to have an orgasm this way is the result of what particular factor in her personal physical make-up?
   a. A very large pudenda
   b. Predisposition to be multiorgasmic
   c. A partner who is skilled at foreplay and masturbation
   d. Where the woman's clitoris is located within the folds of her vagina

Answers to Arousal and Erogenous Zones

1. d. While the brain is the source for all sexual imagination, it's the epidermis, or skin, which is our most sensitive organ. Skin is sensitive; it has thousands and thousands of nerve endings, all rarin' to be stimulated! Stimulating the skin is a primary element of all successful lovemaking because our skin is the trigger for all our sexual feelings and voluptuousness.

2. a. The vagus, otherwise known as the nape of the neck, is a primary erogenous zone for many women, but, oddly enough, not for very many men. Some women can experience a full orgasm from gentle stroking, licking, or sucking of the small area behind the ear and down the nape of the neck. Dangling earrings may be worn to stimulate this area while the woman is walking around, fully clothed. Now you know why so many ladies favor large candelabra-style earrings.

3. b. Tickling can be a very erotic activity. Or it can be a kind of erotic torture! Some people can have an orgasm from being tickled, especially when they are tickled on the soles of their feet. During tickling the skin becomes extra sensitive,

sometimes to the point of being unbearable. There are people who can experience orgasm purely through tickling, which is one of the reasons why hormonally charged adolescent couples who are on the brink of actively exploring their sexuality often engage in long mutual tickling sessions as a "safe sex," ostensibly innocent activity.

4. a. The *Kama Sutra*, a centuries-old, East Indian, all-encompassing guide to courtship and lovemaking translated into English in the late 1880s by F. Arbuthnot and Sir Richard Burton (not the actor), frequently refers to shampooing throughout its many pages. Shampooing then did not mean what it does today, which is the washing of the hair, although if you get a shampoo at an upscale beauty salon, very often the shampoo does include a head and scalp massage. To shampoo someone originally meant to massage or knead anywhere on the body without the presence of soap and water. The head and scalp are notoriously sensitive and charged with nerve endings, making it an ideal place to be massaged. If a little erotic pleasure can be derived from an ordinary shampoo, even one you give yourself or your lover in the shower, why abstain? Go ahead. Lather up!

5. d. A good licking—or lapping, or even sucking—of any portion of any erogenous zone, be it the nape of the neck, the area behind the knees, the furrow between the legs, or the cleft between the breasts, not to mention any or all of the genital area, is certainly the most expedient and easy way to moisten one's own or anyone else's erogenous zone. Just put your wet tongue on it.

6. a. Breathing in, not out, is essential when one is licking or otherwise putting one's nose and mouth very close, if not actu-

ally into, another person's ear. First of all, breathing in will cause a pleasant, slight vacuum to occur inside the other person's ear, resulting in warm, borderline erotic sensations. But breathing out, especially a big exhale, could hurt the other person and even rupture or otherwise damage their eardrum. A forceful gust of air into anyone else's orifice (unless you're giving them mouth-to-mouth CPR) is not a good idea. While you're at it, remember to also breathe in, not out, into anyone's vagina.

7. d. Hickeys—love bites—are caused by blood being raised to the skin by extreme suction of the lips on the epidermis. Hickeys are really caused by an extreme kiss. While some call them a form of decoration and others a form of mutilation, sages of love call hickeys the physical proof of passion's violent nature. But giving someone a hickey can cause trouble. Two unlucky Canadian women actually faced jail time for pinning down a third woman friend and giving her three hickeys on her upper body and legs. One of the women informed the court they were merely teasing the woman about her relationship with a particular man who was serving time in jail. The case was later adjourned.

8. b. The G-Spot, sometimes called the Grafenberg spot in homage to the doctor who claimed to have discovered it, has been likened to an accessory clitoris located just inside the vaginal opening. Some women say the best way to access the G-Spot is not through the vagina, but by deep massage of the mons veneris or just under the pubic bone. Both the G-Spot and the clitoris share a common nerve, and stimulation of one often stimulates the other. Sensitivity varies from woman to woman, but many women claim that a G-Spot orgasm is like no other. More intense, more powerful, possibly just more hooey.

9. d. A few, but not many, women say they get their most profound orgasms as a result of having their mons veneris massaged or when they press their mons veneris up against something. Certainly there are some women who find their mons to be particularly sensitive to external stimulation and who prefer it over the internal digital or even cunnilingual approach.

Statistics, Dimensions, Calculations, and the Art of Measuring It All

It's kind of ridiculous, but we have to face facts. Everybody is interested in size. Some of us are frankly hung up on it! Whether we're talking about the size of a person's breasts, the girth of their hips, or, of course, the mother of all size comparisons, the dimensions of anyone's penis, knowing the precise size of certain organs can obsess and control us, not always to our benefit! In the world of anatomy, especially sexual anatomy, everything is up for measure. Doctors and scientists doing research at recognized institutes of sexual study—the ABS (American Board of Sexology), the NIH (National Institutes of Health), and the Kinsey Institute for Research in Sex, Gender, and Reproduction, to name a few—spend their workday calculating nipple size and counting orgasms. Interesting work if you can get it, no? In the great wide world of sex, numbers can be very revealing.

1. The average penis is how many inches when flaccid?
    a. 5.2 inches
    b. 6.1 inches
    c. 3.5 inches
    d. 2.2 inches

2. What is the average length of an erect penis in full hard-on?
   a. 6.1 inches
   b. 5.5 inches
   c. 6.6 inches
   d. 5.1 inches

3. What's the average span ejaculate can fly?
   a. 7 to 12 inches
   b. 12 to 62 inches
   c. 12 to 24 inches
   d. 8 to 16 inches

4. What are the dimensions of the smallest human penis on record?
   a. 1 centimeter
   b. 1 inch
   c. 0.5 inch
   d. 0.25 inch

5. To increase the length of their penises, men of the Caramoja tribe in northern Uganda tie weights to the ends, while the males of the Mambas tribe of New Hebrides in the tropical Southern Hemisphere have a custom of stretching and then wrapping their penises in yards of cloth to make them longer. Talk about an arduous—not to mention dubious—process! How long can these elongation freaks get their penises to stretch/grow?
   a. 21 inches
   b. 11 inches
   c. 9 inches
   d. 17 inches

6. When polled, women are most likely to say the average length of an erect penis is 4 inches. Men always say something different. What do men say is the average length?
    a. 14 inches
    b. 7 inches
    c. 6 inches
    d. 10 inches

7. What mammal, from the wild and crazy mammal capital Madagascar, has the most known number of nipples on its body?
    a. A lemur
    b. A civet
    c. A mongoose
    d. A tenrac

8. The average unoccupied vagina measures approximately how many inches in length?
    a. 4 inches
    b. 6 inches
    c. Exactly 5.1 inches, the same length as the average-sized penis
    d. 7 inches

9. Hottentot women are known for their awesome posteriors. Their substantial gluteus maximus is regarded as a human genetic variation known as steatopygous. Just how big are Hottentot women's rear ends?
    a. 2–3 feet across
    b. The average is 3 feet wide
    c. 18–24 inches
    d. The same size as J-Lo's

10. A vigorous, get-the-blood-moving, thirty-minute session of lovemaking will burn how many calories?
    a. 250 calories
    b. 500 calories
    c. 150 calories
    d. 50 calories

11. In 1964 topless dancer Carol Doda underwent 20 weeks of silicone treatments to upgrade her bra size from 34 to what?
    a. 40 inches
    b. 38 inches
    c. 46 inches
    d. 44 inches

12. TRUE OR FALSE. Exceptionally large nipples are an indication that a woman's clitoris is exceptionally large, too.

Answers to Statistics, Dimensions, and Calculations

1. c. The average penis before tumescence, that is, prior to erection, is a mere 3.5 inches. Erect, the penis can nearly double in size, which is one of the reasons why some women (usually true penis appreciators) are so fascinated with watching the way erections grow. There are some men whose erect penises don't get much longer as tumescence occurs, but whose penises grow particularly thick. People who are picky about penises claim shorter, thicker penises have their own unique assets, providing a specific pleasure not duplicated by merely long ones.

2. d. The average erect, fully aroused, penis is 5.1 inches in length, a figure that takes into consideration the mean of all men. Naturally, a great many men have penises far longer than

5.1 inches. A good number of them have penises that aren't. Studies have been conducted indicating that nationalities and certain geographical or culturally anthropologic traits may have a great bearing on penis size. The bottom line is that no matter how big a man is, they all say they are bigger.

3. c. Human ejaculate has been documented to fly—be it across the room, into someone's eye, or at a moving target—anywhere from 12 to 24 inches. Sperm can fly pretty far. This is an odd fact, considering that the farthest most sperm gets to fly is the distance between a woman's vagina and her cervix or into someone's sock. That old saw about a woman being impregnated by a man masturbating from across the room might in fact be true, albeit unlikely.

4. a. The smallest adult penis recorded by sex researchers is a mere one centimeter.

5. d. The longest penis recorded by anthropologists studying the Caramoja tribe in northern Uganda as well as the Mambas of New Hebrides is an amazing 17 inches long. In the case of the Mambas, it's really not known just how long any given man's penis is—nobody knows for sure since they're shy about unraveling the yards of cloth. *Ripley's Believe It or Not* reports that the Caramoja guys stretch theirs out so long they have to walk around with them tied up in knots.

6. d. When it comes to hazarding guesses at overall penile statistics, men tend to exaggerate their dimensions. As a rule, the majority of men overestimate the size of everyone's penis, including their own. When polled, most men say they believe the average erect penis measures 10 inches. The question is, are they measuring from the shaft (or root) or from the glans to the

'nads? Penis length differs widely depending on where you're holding the tape measure.

7. d. The tenrac, or tenrec, a hedgehog-like, insect-eating beast native to Madagascar, has the most nipples of any mammal. The average tenrac usually boasts twenty-two to twenty-four nipples on its belly and chest, which is probably the reason why it's called a "ten rack." For the record, lemurs, civets, and mongoose(s) are all animals native to Madagascar.

8. a. Your basic, all-purpose, ordinary, garden-variety vagina measures 4 inches in length. That is why the average 5.1-inch penis is more than adequate to give pleasure and perform its reproductive responsibilities.

9. a. Hottentot women, famous for their posteriors, are the queens, so to speak, of the big-bottom brigade. It's not uncommon for Hottentot women to have butts measuring two to three feet across. While Westerners may consider these outsize behinds to be peculiar, in the land of the Hottentots big butts rule.

10. c. Thirty minutes of vigorous lovemaking burns 150 calories. But if you eat anything except celery after making love, you won't lose any weight from the activity.

11. d. In June 1964, Carol Doda, undisputed star of the topless club scene in San Francisco, spent 20 weeks undergoing silicone treatments, transforming her 34"-26"-36" figure to new, gargantuan proportions. Her bra size catapulted a full five sizes, making her measurements 44"-26"-36". The Bay area girl made headlines a few months later when Lloyds of London insured her new bosom for $1.5 million, probably as a publicity stunt.

12. False. Some women have very large nipples. Some women have very small ones. There is no scientific evidence connecting the size of a woman's nipple with the size of her clitoris, just as there is no scientific evidence that a woman's nipple size will affect the strength or quality of her orgasm.

Masturbation and Orgasm

PEOPLE HAVE BEEN touching themselves for pleasure ever since humans discovered their hands. Masturbation is what comes naturally! It's been shown that humans aren't the only ones to stimulate themselves—ever watch a bored monkey in a monkey house? And since sustained masturbation—for one's own pleasure or for somebody else's—inevitably leads to orgasm, it makes sense that the two go hand in hand (or hand on genitalia). That's why these two essential portions of the quiz are always linked together!

Masturbation . . . Can Be Fun

Do you beat off, whack the willy, play with your pudenda, stimulate yourself? Fun, isn't it? Test your knowledge about an activity you might regularly engage in, especially if you're young and randy!

1. TRUE OR FALSE. The average woman has a preference for masturbating either to the left or to the right side of her vagina.

2. TRUE OR FALSE. The more frequently a woman masturbates, the less time it takes for her to bring herself to orgasm.

3. According to Masters and Johnson, masturbation can help alleviate what common female ailment?
   a. Sore breasts
   b. Pelvic cramping and backaches
   c. Yeast infections
   d. PID (Pelvic Inflammatory Disease)

4. Readers of Alfred Kinsey's 1953 study, *Sexual Behavior in the Human Female*, learned that what percentage of women masturbated themselves to orgasm using only thigh pressure?
   a. 14 percent
   b. 10 percent
   c. 30 percent
   d. 2 percent

5. What episode of *Seinfeld* won an Emmy award for its hilarious depiction of masturbation?
   a. "The Outing"
   b. "The Contest"
   c. "The Stakeout"
   d. "The Glasses"

6. The average age that males begin to ejaculate is:
   a. Between the ages of 10 and 16
   b. Between the ages of 11 and 12
   c. Between the ages of 12 and 15
   d. Between the ages of 18 and 20

7. Hysterical opposition to masturbation dates back centuries, although it reached its prudish apex in the 19th century. Which culture strongly condemned masturbation, at times making it punishable by death?
   a. The Christians
   b. The Greeks
   c. The Hebrews
   d. The Romans

8. What larger-than-life personality, educator, and contemporary author has been colloquially referred to as "The Mother of All Masturbators"?
   a. Madonna
   b. Betty Dodson
   c. Nancy Friday
   d. Rosie O'Donnell

9. Erectile tissue is found in only three parts of the human body. One is the chest, another is the genitals. What is the third?
   a. The nose
   b. The neck
   c. The ears
   d. The facial lips

10. TRUE OR FALSE. A person can masturbate when he or she is sleeping.

Answers to Masturbation . . . Can Be Fun

1. True. According to Masters and Johnson, most women concentrate on one side of their clitoral shaft: the right side if they are right-handed, the left side if they are lefties. Women rarely manipulate the head of the clitoris directly when they masturbate. It's too sensitive and the sensation can be too intense and irritating to the clitoris. Every woman develops her own masturbation style, and there's no right way or wrong way to do it. Whatever gets you off is the correct way.

2. True. The more often you masturbate, the more tuned-in to your body's responses you become. Frequent masturbation cuts down on the time needed for getting to orgasm. Female masturbators can train the body for multiple orgasms the way a runner can train the body to endure miles of running. Long and frequent masturbation sessions can lead to longer and more orgasmic lovemaking, so ladies, masturbate to your heart's content.

3. b. In their 1966 study, *Human Sexual Response*, Masters and Johnson discovered that women who masturbated to the point of orgasm shortly after the start of their menstrual cycle experienced far less of the pelvic cramping and backache associated with menstruation. Whether it's due to the increased flow of blood to the area being pulsated by the rolling waves of pleasure caused by orgasm, or something a bit more psychological, it's true. The old wives' tale that masturbation can get rid of cramps is more than just a tale.

4. b. According to Kinsey's 1953 study, *Sexual Behavior in the Human Female*, a full ten percent of women who masturbated themselves to climax used only the friction generated from rubbing together their thighs to achieve orgasm. Riding horses

works, too, but the thigh-rubbing, no-hands plan works great at any desk or office.

5. b. An episode of *Seinfeld* called "The Contest" won an Emmy award for the 1992–93 season. The theme of the episode was masturbation. The plotline is that Jerry challenges George, Kramer, and Elaine to see "who can hold out longest" from pleasuring him- or herself.

6. c. According to the Sexual Health Info Center, an on-line guide to sexual health, the average age that males begin to ejaculate is between the ages of 12 and 15. Most males masturbate, often for years, before they are able to ejaculate. The ability to ejaculate, which is connected to the hormonal changes of puberty, arrives for different males at different times.

7. c. At one time, the Hebrews had such a strong proscription against the practice of masturbation that anyone caught in the act doing it was liable to be executed. The prohibition against self-pleasuring did not die out with older cultures. It is still quite illegal to be caught masturbating in most portions of the United States.

8. b. Betty Dodson, an outspoken advocate for masturbation since 1970, has been colloquially called "The Mother of All Masturbators." Dodson, who started out running workshops for women to teach them how to masturbate, became the writer, producer, and sometimes star of a line of educational videotapes focusing on masturbation. In 2002, Dodson authored a book called *Orgasms For Two*, and in 2003, came out with her follow-up book, *Sex For One: The Joy of Selfloving*, a book that sings the praises of self-pleasuring and advises readers to make time to take a masturbation break every day.

9. a. The nose contains erectile tissue, which is why flared nostrils are a sign of sexual interest. The only other parts of the human body which contain erectile tissue are the chest and the genitalia.

10. True. A person not only can masturbate while asleep, but can have an orgasm, too. Amazingly, he or she might not remember any of it in the morning!

The Big O

Very few subjects have enjoyed the scrutiny and popularity of orgasm, or "The Big O," as many of the editors of ladies' and lad magazines choose to call it. Orgasm (known in France as "la petite mort," or "little death," a rather morbid metaphor for orgasm if you stop and think about it) is defined by the Merriam-Webster dictionary as "the climax of sexual excitement." Although the word orgasm gives some people the giggles and is often associated with something vaguely smarmy, orgasm is actually the endgame of a complex system of nerve endings and physiological responses, best understood by medical experts and sex researchers. Most of us just want to come . . . and come often! In this portion of the quiz, you will test your knowledge of orgasm, and hopefully make some discoveries about your most intimate self.

1. TRUE OR FALSE. Most woman don't require penetration to get off and can be brought to orgasm by massaging or kneading the mons pubis.

2. Monica Lewinsky must not have been aware of this simple cleaning trick. As any respectable housekeeper knows, it's

possible to remove semen stains from clothing or furniture by using what easily found cleaning tool?

a. Any bleach-based cleanser

b. Vinegar and water

c. A diluted solution of sodium bicarbonate

d. The product Shout

3. According to the anonymous female author of *The Sensuous Woman*, a sexual how-to manual published in 1971, occasionally faking an orgasm is not only an acceptable but desirable practice, essential to the well-being of any long-term relationship. But the author advises women against telling a man, no matter how annoyed she is with him, that she's ever pretended in bed. Why should the faking of an orgasm never be revealed?

a. According to the author, all men suspect women sometimes fake it, but it's pointless to tell them what they already know

b. According to the author, men should be lied to on a regular basis no matter what the topic is

c. According to the author, to do so would be to betray an inviolable trust shared by every woman in the world

d. According to the author, most men wouldn't recognize a genuine female orgasm from a fake one if they got hit over the head with one

4. The belief that simultaneous orgasm is the only way for two people to reach authentic sexual fulfillment is:

a. Egregiously erroneous

b. True

c. True, with caveats

d. If they're really in love, two people will always reach their climax at the same time

5. The average human orgasm lasts only a few seconds. Some animals have orgasms that last for many minutes. What animal has an orgasm that can last for 30 minutes?
   a. Cat
   b. Pig
   c. Cow
   d. Rabbit

6. What is the single most important factor explaining why older women have an easier time orgasming than younger women?
   a. The more sexually experienced a woman is, the more fine tuned her body becomes at achieving a sexual climax
   b. Multiple births and expansion of the birth canal increase a woman's ability to have an orgasm
   c. Older women are naturally hornier
   d. Older women are less inhibited about getting what they need to achieve orgasm

7. TRUE OR FALSE. Laughing during sex is good for enhancing and increasing the number of orgasms.

8. TRUE OR FALSE. From a physiological point of view, not all female orgasms are the same.

Answers to The Big O

1. True. The mythology that women require penetration to achieve orgasm is just that: a myth. The great majority of females first experience orgasm long before they start having intercourse or inserting objects, including their own fingers, into

their vaginas. Most females discover the pleasurable sensations of orgasm accidentally, almost always because something—even their own clothing—is rubbing against their genitals. External massaging or kneading of the labia and entire pubic area or mons pubis is sufficient for the majority of women to achieve orgasm, if the massaging or kneading generates enough friction and continues long enough.

2. c. A simple solution of sodium bicarbonate, also known as baking soda, is a cleaning agent found in many people's homes (try looking in the refrigerator . . . that's where most people keep the Arm & Hammer) that will quickly and easily remove semen stains. Baking soda is useful for removing other stains as well, including coffee and tobacco stains from one's teeth.

3. c. The author of *The Sensuous Woman*, an epic how-to-make-love tome, said there are some secrets each sex should never reveal to the other. The one about sometimes faking orgasm is one of them.

4. a. A great deal of propaganda exists in marriage manuals, sex advice columns, and stuff you see in movies regarding the significance of the simultaneous orgasm. Sure, it's great if you come together. Some couples who are really attuned to each other's bodies and who have been making love together for some time can teach their bodies to respond in ways that make simultaneous orgasm more likely. But it is a huge mistake to think that if you don't come together that something is wrong. Sometimes it's fun and informative to have your orgasm and then watch your partner have theirs. People's facial expressions during orgasm can be quite revealing! Come together if you can, but enjoy the other person's orgasm if you don't.

5. b. Pigs can have orgasms lasting up to thirty minutes, although a ten-minute pig orgasm is far more common. Lucky pigs! But it's also physically impossible for pigs to look up into the sky.

6. a. The more sexually experienced a woman is, the easier it is for her body to coordinate and process all the reflexes and nervous system responses necessary to generate orgasm. Young women frequently experience difficulty in reaching a climax, mostly because their bodies and minds are not experienced enough to coordinate all the diverse elements necessary to achieve orgasm. The more sex a woman has, the better her body becomes at enjoying it. Sex is certainly one activity where practice really pays off.

7. True. Sex and laughing both produce in the body endorphins, the natural chemical substances that reduce pain, relieve stress, and increase the state of euphoria. Laughing in bed actually releases a double dose of the hormones responsible for feeling good. So go ahead and laugh in bed—just not at your partner!

8. True. Women who are very attuned to their bodies describe being able to have three different types of orgasm: clitoral, vaginal, and a combination of the two. During a clitoral orgasm, the vagina is believed to slightly lengthen, resulting in a pocket forming beneath the uterus. During a vaginal orgasm, the uterus drops slightly, making the vagina shorter. Stimulation of both the vagina and the clitoris can cause a blended orgasm, which, depending on the individual, may be the most intense orgasm of the three.

Aphrodisiacs

APHRODISIACS—from aromatic recipes and potions to the sensual and sexual enhancers found in nature—have been in existence for thousands of years. The ancient Greeks and Romans were famously hedonistic, as were the Taoist Chinese and the Tantric Hindus. Today people use aromatic oils and eat certain foods in the interest of generating more sexual pleasure. Thousands of years ago lovers anointed their bodies to enhance their senses just as modern lovers anoint their bodies today. Aphrodisiacs are agents that excite sexual desire. Test your knowledge about them now!

1. Which ancient goddess is said to be the governor of perfumery, sensuality, massage, and cosmetics?
   a. Artemis
   b. Aphrodite
   c. Athena
   d. Demeter

2. In India, a nation that reveres the sex organs (the Indian god Shiva and his powerful penis or *lingam* are believed to have brought the world to existence), perfumes easily travel back and forth from the temple to the bedchamber. What is India's most famous perfume for inspiring physical love?
   a. Sandalwood
   b. Patchouli
   c. Jonquil
   d. Hyacinth

3. Cardamom, black pepper, cloves, and cinnamon are every-
   day spices found in the average American kitchen cabinet,
   but in India many people consider them to be:
   a. Bad for sex
   b. Sleep-inducing
   c. Calming elements
   d. Aphrodisiacs

4. The most famous of all the Brazilian aphrodisiacs is a plant
   whose reputation has spread far and wide for being a libido
   enhancer. What is this famous aphrodisiacal plant?
   a. Yohimbe
   b. Marapuama
   c. Catuaba
   d. Damiana

5. The inner shavings of the bark of a certain kind of tree
   have been ingested by male members of Bantu-speaking
   tribes of West Central Africa to help them last longer
   during mating rituals. What is the active ingredient that can
   be gleaned from the bark of this tree?
   a. Great Kapok
   b. Yohimbe
   c. Selenium
   d. Mahogany

6. What is it about oysters that gives them their reputation for
   being an aphrodisiac?
   a. They give eaters a protein rush.
   b. They contain high levels of zinc.
   c. They are a quick meal that won't fill you up to the
       point where you only want to go to sleep and skip
       making love.

    d. Oysters equal horny in many people's minds . . . it's subliminal seduction.

7. Why do so many types of seafood have an aphrodisiacal association?
    a. Because so many seafoods are a source of iron, and iron puts wood in the old mallet.
    b. Because seafood smells are also associated, for better or worse, with the female genital region (hence the famous "smells like fish" line).
    c. Because the goddess Aphrodite was said to be born from the sea.
    d. Because seafood comes from the water, and water is associated with wetness.

8. What famous aphrodisiacal food contains large amounts of vitamins and phosphorus?
    a. Caviar
    b. Quail eggs
    c. Olives
    d. Goose liver

9. In Greek myth, which plant was chosen by the goddess Aphrodite to cover her nakedness? It has been associated with modest sensuality ever since.
    a. The rose
    b. The geranium
    c. The myrtle
    d. Clary sage

10. Damiana, an overall tonic herb easily found in any health-food store, is treasured by many cultures for its reputed curative powers for men suffering from low sex drive,

impotence, premature ejaculation, and prostate discharges. Damiana is also recommended for women who suffer from what ailment?

a. Low sex drive

b. PMS

c. Chronic fatigue

d. Dry vagina

11. What plant readily found in the Third World is taken to improve male libido and erection?

a. *Celosia argentea*, or "Cock's Comb"

b. Marijuana

c. Marapuama

d. Oleander

12. To achieve sexual fulfillment, a therapeutic douche can be made with which following ingredients?

a. Clary sage, geranium, jasmine, patchouli, and spring water

b. Lavender, bergamot, ravansara, and tea tree

c. Lemongrass, juniper, ylang ylang, and jojoba

d. Clove, cypress, neroli, and chamomile

13. What zero-calorie vegetable is actually considered to be an aphrodisiac?

a. Lettuce

b. Celery

c. Cucumber

d. Radish

14. What fruit of the maidenhair tree resembles a persimmon in color, size, and character with one unique exception?

a. Macadamia nuts

b. Vengurla nuts

    c. Chintamani nuts

    d. Gingko nuts

15. To enhance vaginal lubrication, a woman can rub a little of what kind of oil into and onto her vagina to slick it up?
    a. Wintergreen
    b. Lavender
    c. Jojoba
    d. Bergamot

16. Tea tree or lavender oil dribbled on a tampon (before it's in the body but after it's been removed from its protective wrapper) is recommended for what purpose?
    a. To enhance the feminine libido
    b. To make the vagina less odiferous
    c. To cure a noninfectious vaginal discharge
    d. To increase fertility

17. What spice has been used for thousands of years to excite the senses, but which if ingested in large amounts will have you running for the bathroom?
    a. Nutmeg
    b. Ginger
    c. Clove
    d. Horseradish

18. Rubbing one's penis with a special butter made from buffalo fat will cause the penis to:
    a. Temporarily grow bigger
    b. Temporarily become harder
    c. Be able to provide pleasure to two women
    d. Experience multiple orgasms

19. What fruit is said to be capable of causing sexual intoxication?
    a. A pomegranate
    b. A thorn apple
    c. A kiwi
    d. A strawberry

20. Milk, mixed with sugar and the boiled testicle of a goat or a ram, promises to have which of the following results when eaten?
    a. You will be able to have nonstop sex for hours.
    b. Your penis will grow bigger.
    c. You will be able to stave off ejaculation.
    d. You will realize a remarkable increase in sexual vigor.

21. What essential oil is helpful for solving sexual problems of all stripes?
    a. Neroli
    b. Mandarin
    c. China Rose
    d. Ylang Ylang

22. Why did ancient Romans throw walnuts instead of rice at weddings?
    a. They wanted to hurt the bridal couple so they would understand right away the pain of marriage.
    b. Walnuts were, and are still, believed to hold powers of fertility.
    c. Eating walnuts was believed to make a man hard.
    d. Because a split-open walnut resembles the female vulva.

23. TRUE OR FALSE. We may be attracted or put off by someone just because of their smell.

24. What is "Spanish fly"?
    a. An topical ointment said to drive women into a state of sexual frenzy
    b. A sex-crazed bug from South America
    c. An aphrodisiac made from bugs said to induce sexual arousal
    d. There is no such thing as Spanish fly

25. What combination of essential oils is said to have been a favorite among 19th-century prostitutes to increase their fortune and ensure financial gain?
    a. Cinnamon, musk, and juniper
    b. Vanilla, rose, and jasmine
    c. Vetavert, frangipani, and lavender
    d. Belladonna, hemlock, and opium

Answers to Aphrodisiacs

1. b. Aphrodite is believed to be the goddess of perfumery, sensuality, massage—and all things aesthetic and joyful. The word "aphrodisiac" comes from her name. Aphrodite is a popular goddess in the lore of aromatherapy, which is the art of healing perfumery. Aromatherapists suggest the use of aromatic oils that can be applied to the skin or inhaled through a diffuser to heighten the senses and enhance the sexual experience. Specific oils and tinctures are used to get in touch with the sexual elements of the psyche.

2. a. While patchouli has its admirers (and seriously puts off everyone else), sandalwood is the most famous of all the perfumes for love. The Hindu god Indra is always represented with

his breast painted with the oil. Sandalwood is recommended for sensual massage, energizing massage, care of the breast, and for a shallow bath meant to soothe inflamed genitals—the last not a bad thing to take after a protracted bout of love. On the subject of breasts, aromatherapists who are into aphrodisia sometimes advise women with small breasts to massage them with a clary sage, geranium, and ylang ylang mixture added to a camellia base. Doing this every night, they say, will increase the size and tone of one's breasts.

3. d. In the Indian culture, cardamom, black pepper, cloves, and cinnamon are considered to be aphrodisiacs. Blended into a spicy tea made with sugar and hot milk, clove, cardamom, cinnamon, and black pepper happen to be the ingredients for "Chai" tea, a popular coffee and tea bar drink. And you thought it was just a trendy coffee bar–type beverage!

4. c. Catuaba is the most famous of all the Brazilian aphrodisiacs for its reputation as a libido enlivener for men. Homeopathic healers advise using it in combination with marapuama to stimulate the male sexual and urinary organs and to prevent impotence. One of catuaba's more unusual side effects is the production of magnificent erotic dreams.

5. b. Yohimbe, derived from the tree *Corynanthe yohimbe*, enjoys a reputation for being a cure for erection disorders and impotence. Bantu-speaking users claim Yohimbe works wonders for increasing stamina at their tribal mating rituals, which can go on for 15 days. Yohimbe, or some diluted or distilled version of yohimbe, can be bought at health food stores. Yohimbe is said to work by stimulating chemical reactions in the body aiding blood flow to the sex organs.

6. b. It is true: Oysters are protein, they are a quick meal that won't make you feel stuffed, and they are equated with horniness in most people's minds. However, oysters are truly the food of love because of their high levels of zinc. Zinc has been clinically proven to improve the sex drive.

7. c. The goddess Aphrodite is said to have been born from the sea, the cradle of life.

8. a. The eggs of the sturgeon, better known as caviar, in fact contain large amounts of vitamins A, D, B_1, B_2, and B_6, and phosphorus, all of which are known stimulants to the system.

9. c. The myrtle plant was chosen by Aphrodite to shield her nakedness, and myrtle has been associated with the goddess of love ever since. Terribly out of fashion now, Myrtle was once considered to be a tantalizing name. It would be on par with naming your daughter "Venus" today. Indulging in a bath scented with myrtle oil in a dim, quiet room is recommended to cleanse, soothe, and inspire a woman into believing that she is a goddess—and ready to make love with her god.

10. b. Damiana is frequently prescribed by homeopathic doctors as a cure for PMS. It is also said to work well for menopause, but since the symptoms of menopause (vaginal dryness, mood swings, hot flashes, and irregular menstrual cycle) can last for up to ten years, a woman might be taking a lot of Damiana.

11. c. The herb marapuama, which sounds like marijuana but is not, has a long and famous history as a powerful aphrodisiac. Cultivated for centuries in many Third World Hispanic cultures, marapuama is prized for improving the male libido and causing

sturdier erections. It can also be taken in tea as a remedy for exhaustion and is said to relieve insomnia and hypertension.

12. b. Up to ten drops of any or a combination of all of the following ingredients—lavender, bergamot, ravansara, and tea tree—mixed with 100 ml of spring water is said to be the recipe for achieving sexual fulfillment when used as a douche. These ingredients are also handy for clearing up any irritation caused by an overabundance of lovemaking.

13. b. Celery has a reputation for being an aphrodisiac and has a long history of being a food of love. Celery contains vitamins A, C, B, D, and lots of minerals. Its seeds more than the stalky growth are said to be aphrodisiacal. Sprinkle some around and see what comes up.

14. d. Gingko nuts are the fruit of the maidenhair tree, or *Gingko biloba*. Raw, the flesh of the fruit has an exceptionally foul scent. Prepared Gingko nuts, however, are delicious, especially in a Japanese custard soup called *chawanmushi*. The Japanese use it for making a kidney tonic for men reputed to increase sexual energy, stop incontinence—and even restore hearing loss. In the West, the whole nuts can be bought canned, or dried in capsules. In parts of the U.S. the maidenhair tree grows on city streets, throwing off the foul-smelling fruit that only clever old Asian women will pick up.

15. c. Jojoba oil applied directly to the vagina is believed to be a natural lubricant that works well for most women. Oil of camellia is said to be of great benefit as well.

16. c. While perfuming a tampon with tea tree or lavender oil will undoubtedly cause a woman's—particularly a menstruating

woman's—vagina to have an improved aroma, its purpose is not to counter stinky syndrome, but to cure a noninfectious vaginal discharge. While tea tree or lavender oil are not considered to be actual love enhancers, certainly anything that makes the vagina more enticing and appealing has aphrodisiacal merit.

17. b. Ginger has been used as an aphrodisiac to spike drinks for centuries. Judiciously used in tiny amounts, it causes a slight hot flush; give your date too much and she'll be spending the night in the bathroom.

18. a. Rubbing the penis with butter made from the fat of a buffalo is thought to cause the penis to grow bigger. The swelling is the result of irritation caused by mild allergic reaction—and can last up to a month.

19. b. A thorn apple, if you can find one (they still grow them in Peru), is said to cause sexual intoxication. References to the apple and its ability to drive women into a passionate frenzy can be traced back to the story of Adam and Eve in the Garden of Eden. It was eating the apple (a thorn apple?) that made the couple so horny and ruined the innocence of the Garden.

20. d. In the East Indian culture, imbibing a beverage of milk, sugar, and the boiled testicle of a goat or a ram—now is that a whole testicle, or just parts?—is said to provide stamina and great sexual vigor. But first you have to catch the ram or the goat.

21. d. Ylang Ylang, an essential oil rendered from the flower of the same name, and which means "Flower of flowers," is reputed to be a sexual healer. The best oil comes from the yellow flowers, although the plants bloom in shades of pink, mauve, and

yellow. Ylang Ylang slows down the pulse and steadies an irregular heartbeat due to stress. Ylang Ylang is said to work prima-
rily, however, on the emotions, and is a natural anti-depressant.
Calming and soothing, it is also a natural relaxant.

22. b. The ancient Romans believed walnuts, now recognized
to be a powerful source of vitamins and minerals, to be vital to
a strong immune system. Walnuts were believed to hold the
powers of fertility, and to throw walnuts at a marrying couple
was to wish them great luck at conceiving and bearing children.

23. True. Without knowing it, we communicate sexual attraction to each other in some degree by scent. Pheromones, a word
that comes from the Greek word for "excitement," are the substance naturally produced by one person that provokes a
response from another. Pheromones are an invitation to mate
and are secreted by the sex glands in vaginal secretions, and
saliva and through the skin. Most people are unaware of how
their scent influences another person's passion, except for the
French who have an expression that literally means "I can't stand
his smell."

24. c. Spanish fly, which is a powder made from pulverized
blister-beetles, contains cantharides, which can cause physical
arousal, sort of, by irritating the urinary tract when ingested and
excreted. According to a book called *Aphrodisiacs: The Science
and the Myth*, Spanish fly was used in the mid-19th century to
treat pleurisy. But Spanish fy can be dangerous. In Victorian
England several cases of manslaughter or malicious poisoning by
Spanish fly were reported. More recently, the active ingredients
in Spanish fly have been used medicinally to dissolve external
warts.

25. b. A mixture of vanilla, rose, and jasmine (combined with a bit of coral and some gold glitter) was said to be a favorite recipe of 19th-century prostitutes who wished to improve business. Mixing these ingredients was said to create a recipe called "Follow Me Boy." The concoction was rubbed on the woman's body and was believed to be an irresistible aphrodisiac.

Lubes and Toys

FAR REMOVED from the procreative aspects of sex (biology may be destiny, but if you're working overtime to become pregnant, sex can be a bore), to help keep sex interesting, many people enjoy sex toys and games. This fascinating portion of the quiz tests your knowledge of lubricants and toys and may give you some good ideas about how to incorporate them into your own erotic adventures.

Lubes

Lubricants, or "lubes," are the most basic of sexual enhancers. They keep things wet, reduce friction, and keep moving parts moving. Just about anything—except elbow grease—can be used as a lubricant. Test your knowledge about natural and artificial lubricants and use your knowledge to enhance your own personal experiences.

1. Lubricants come in two formulas, water based and oil based. A primary objection to water-based lubes is that they:
   a. Have a medicinal taste
   b. Dry up too fast
   c. Are expensive
   d. Cannot be purchased "over the counter"

2. TRUE OR FALSE. Lube is always needed for any anal activity.

3. Water-based lubes engineered specifically for anal sex differ from other water-based lubes in what regard?
   a. They always include an antibacterial agent
   b. They're thicker, more like hair goo
   c. They are scented
   d. They're ill advised for use with condoms

4. The most popular and available lube used among gay men is reputed to be:
   a. Wesson oil
   b. Peanut oil
   c. Spit
   d. The vegetable shortening Crisco

5. Popular and easily accessible lubes such as petroleum jelly and baby oil have a fatal flaw as sexual lubricants. What is it?
   a. They rub off on clothing and leave stains
   b. They break down latex and allow pinholes to develop in barrier equipment such as gloves, dental dams, and condoms
   c. They're difficult to wash out or get off the skin
   d. They should not be used by people who suffer from allergies

6. Petroleum oil-based lubricants should never be used on what part of the body?
   a. The vagina
   b. The mouth
   c. The breasts
   d. Any epidermis

7. What is the main ingredient found in commercial penile desensitizers, products meant to slow a guy down so he doesn't ejaculate before his partner is ready?
   a. Lidocaine
   b. Benzocaine
   c. Peroxide
   d. Isopropyl alcohol

Answers to Lubricants

1. b. Water-based lubricants do have a tendency to dry up very quickly, but this problem can be solved by adding a little bit of water or saliva.

2. True. The anus is somewhat stretchy and resilient, but it does not secrete much lubrication. The anus may feel somewhat moist if one is experimenting with a finger probe, but that moisture is not true wetness, but mucous secretion. Anal sex requires a lubricant to facilitate entry and prevent delicate tissue from tearing. Lubricant is necessary when engaging in anal sex with a nonlubricated condom to avoid too much friction on thin anal tissue. Just make sure to use a latex-friendly lubricant.

3. b. Thicker lubes provide the additional lubrication necessary for anal sex use. They also have a very different consistency than the usual water-based lubes; actually, in texture, they resemble hair-gel products meant to be used on the head.

4. d. The longtime and much beloved vegetable shortening Crisco has long been a favorite lube among gay men. Cheap and readily available at any supermarket, another plus for Crisco is that since it's vegetable based, it easily flushes out of the body and leaves behind no residue.

5. b. Oil-based lubricants are death to latex. It is a common and potentially fatal disaster to use them in conjunction with condoms, dental dams, gloves, or any other contraceptive/safe-sex equipment for more than a few minutes.

6. a. Petroleum oil-based lubricants should never be used in or around the vagina because they're nearly impossible to wash out and provide an ideal host environment for bacteria and viruses.

7. b. The main ingredient in commercial penile desensitizers sold on-line and in sex shops is benzocaine, which has a mild numbing effect on the epidermis. Most commercial penile desensitizing products, such as Dr. Willy's Penile Desensitizer, for example, contain a 7.5 percent solution of benzocaine that usually results in reducing tactile sensitivity, something that is desirable to men who are concerned about early ejaculation.

Toys

When glossy sex boutiques began popping up in the 1970s in New York City, San Francisco, and Montreal, the sex toy business was revolutionized as the products began to be marketed to couples. Suddenly, middle-aged masturbators and playboy gay guys weren't the only ones interested in anal beads. Lovers everywhere, and of every description, embraced the products. More currently, some of the first retail success stories on the Internet were sites selling sex toys, known as "accessories" by the trade. Call them anything you like—as long as you have fun with them!

1. What is the name of the round-shaped toy meant to be inserted in the rectum for added anal pleasure?
   a. Ben wa balls
   b. An anal plug
   c. Vibrating beads
   d. Bopping Buddies

2. What is the primary purpose of a cock ring?
   a. To enhance the girth of the penis while it is lodged in someone's rectum or vagina.
   b. S&M dominants like to wear them as a symbol of their position.
   c. To support the penis and keep it from wilting.
   d. The ring serves a decorative purpose only.

3. What is a Glow-Daddy?
   a. A man wearing a sparkle-encrusted rubber
   b. A condom that glows in the dark
   c. A black light–responsive dildo
   d. A reflecting condom

4. If you can't find your nipple clamps, what common household item can be used instead?
   a. Napkin rings
   b. Clothespins
   c. Paperclips
   d. Tweezers

5. What sex toy/device is a favorite of women playing the role of a man, or by men who are experiencing temporary or long-term problems with impotence?
   a. Rough Skin Series Groaner, Gripper, Gravitator, and Gyrator
   b. Strap-On Sally
   c. Stormy Slapper
   d. Rubber Head Harness with Muzzle

6. While they were engaged in the act of love, the Indian king of the Panchalas accidentally killed the famous courtesan Madhavasena using what ancient sex toy?
   a. The blindfold
   b. The wedge
   c. Chains
   d. A scarf

7. What is a "clit kisser"?
   a. A vibrator shaped like a tongue and mouth
   b. A flavored water-based lubricant meant to be applied directly to the clitoris
   c. A sex toy that works as a penetrating probe
   d. A vibrator shaped like a tiny penis

8. What essential piece of S&M equipment is hard as a girder, covered in black leather, and topped off with metallic studs?
   a. The rack
   b. A bend-over silicone starter harness kit
   c. The binding board
   d. A paddle

Answers to Toys

1. c. Plastic vibrating beads are an improvement on the old-fashioned traditional porcelain or wooden beads. Why? They're easy to insert and easy to clean, plus the vibrations pleasantly pulsate. Speed can usually be adjusted on vibrating models.

2. c. A cock ring is like an underwire bra for male genitals. It's good for holding things up. Although cock rings make a penis seem wider and S&M dominants favor them for psychological purposes, the primary purpose of a cock ring is to support the penis and to keep it from wilting, especially under heavy use.

3. c. A Glow-Daddy is a black light–responsive dildo with a ribbed and studded shaft. Dildos and battery-powered vibrators come in all shapes and sizes and some incorporate extra enhancements, such as illumination. Great if you're making love in a cave . . . or dungeon, for that matter.

4. b. Clothespins make handy nipple clamps for those who enjoy giving and receiving specialized breast attention. An assortment of black rubber clothespins designed specifically for the purpose are available for purchase in many adult toy stores and, of course, on the Internet.

5. b. Strap-On Sally, as the device is called, is an artificial penis (dildo) attached either by webbing, chains, or straps to either a belt or a body harness. The device or marital aid or sex toy (all and any of these descriptions are correct) is a boon to men who want to engage in coitus with their partners even if their penises won't cooperate. Women who are playing the role of the man in bed also use them. Two women may play with a strap-on or a woman can wear one to anally penetrate a man.

6. b. The wedge, an ancient instrument of love used for prying something apart and keeping it that way, was the sex toy that killed the famous Madhavasena while she was making love with the Indian king of the Panchalas. One can only imagine the anguish of the king when he realized he had killed his lover. The wedge, thankfully, has gone out of favor as a modern-day sex toy.

7. a. A clit kisser is a vibrator that is shaped like a tongue and mouth. The soft plastic jelly "tongue" and "lips" are pulsated by a vibrating egg that artificially creates the sensation of licking, flicking, and kissing. Women can wear this device in their underwear all day to make believe they are being orally serviced by a lover.

8. d. Any dominant worthy of the name must possess a sturdy paddle, the better to spank the pathetic submissive with. Seriously sexy and totally punishing, a paddle is a must-have piece of equipment for any spanking fan.

Oral Sex

THERE ARE MANY exciting and pleasurable activities people can do with their mouths and tongues. According to Bill Clinton, oral sex isn't even "sex." Often referred to as "munching," "eating out," "going down on," as well as other colorful slang descriptions, fellatio (oral sex performed on a penis) and cunnilingus (oral sex performed on a vagina) are not just foreplay, but can be completely realized sex acts in and of themselves. Forgoing other kinds of intercourse and sticking to oral sex will definitely help you stay a virgin! But don't be misled. Just because oral sex isn't intercourse doesn't mean it isn't sophisticated—and very rewarding as a sexual activity!

1. Who invented the Butterfly Flick and what is it?
    a. Erica Jong invented it. The Butterfly Flick is an oral technique involving the mouth, a penis, and an insect.
    b. Camille Paglia invented it as a method for punishing men.
    c. An anonymous woman calling herself "J." invented it as an alternative to the more ordinary blowjob.
    d. Andrea Dworkin came up with the Butterfly Flick and it is a lesbian oral activity.

2. Describe the Silken Swirl.
    a. You put a big mouthful of chocolate mousse in your mouth and your lover pile-drives his penis into it. Men go nuts for this.
    b. You lick the penis up and down after you've dipped your tongue into a bowl of warm honey. Men go nuts for this.
    c. You lick the head and the shaft of the penis over and over in a clockwise and then counterclockwise position using your tongue to aggressively massage the penis. Men go nuts for this.
    d. You grasp only the head and glans of the penis in your mouth and then run your tongue hard all over it. Men go nuts for this.

3. What is a special East Indian name for oral sex?
    a. Dharma
    b. Auparishtaka
    c. Pithamarda
    d. Babhravya

4. When someone puts half of another person's penis in her or his mouth and then forcibly sucks it and kisses it, this is called in East Indian lovemaking:
    a. Nominal congress
    b. Low congress
    c. The Holy Writ
    d. Sucking the mango fruit

5. According to the famous ancient East Indian sex and lovemaking manual, the *Kama Sutra*, these men should refrain from receiving oral sex:

a. Married men
b. Grandfathers
c. The sons of ministers
d. Learned Brahmins and ministers of state

6. What natural instinct must an oral sex lover overcome in order to give his or her partner the ultimate fellatio experience?
   a. To spit out the semen
   b. The gag reflex
   c. The instinct to bite down
   d. To swallow

7. TRUE OR FALSE. A shaved female pubic area is considered more enticing to men for oral sex.

8. TRUE OR FALSE. If you have asparagus for dinner, your urine and your semen will have a strong, medicinal taste.

9. Eating what fruit will actually make semen taste good?
   a. Peaches
   b. Watermelon
   c. Passion fruit
   d. Kiwi

10. Pearl diving, canyon yodeling, and box lunch are all crude synonyms to describe the act known as:
    a. Fellatio
    b. Cunnilingus
    c. Sodomy
    d. Penilingus

Answers to Oral Sex

1. c. It's been said that the how-to writer "J." was not an exceptionally attractive person, at least not physically. What she made up for in lack of looks was her sexual wisdom. Heralded as a "modern Aphrodite" when *The Sensuous Woman* came out, "J." reveals the secret of possibly her most famous invention, the Butterfly Flick, on page 120 of the original edition (a dog-eared page if you can still find a copy). Here, she explains how to lightly pummel the area just beneath the corona of a man's penis with one's tongue. The author likened the movement to tongue strumming a banjo Flick, flick, flick, she advised, until the owner of the penis begs for mercy.

2. c. Any of the above answers sound good enough for you to try at home and you can make up your own name, but the technical answer to this question is c. The Silken Swirl is an oral sex technique conceived of and so named by the famous J., author of *The Sensuous Woman*.

3. b. The giving of oral sex in the Kama Sutra is an act restricted, for the most part, to eunuchs. Two kinds of eunuchs are described in the *Kama Sutra*, those who are dressed as men and those who are dressed as women. Oral sex acts performed in the mouths of eunuchs are called Auparishtaka, or Mouth Congress. Unchaste and wanton women also performed Auparishtaka, but a respectable married lady was never expected to do anything so untoward with her mouth.

4. d. Sucking the mango fruit is but one of the many acts of Auparishtaka that a eunuch or unchaste unmarried woman might perform in the way of oral sex. Nibbling the sides of the penis, pressing it inside, rubbing and pretending to sword swal-

low it are other things that can also be done to a penis with a mouth and a tongue.

5. d. The Auparishtaka or mouth congress, should be avoided by learned Brahmins and ministers of state. In fact, any man of good reputation was instructed to avoid congress with eunuchs or unchaste women for the sake of their good name.

6. b. The gag reflex must be overcome to give a "deep throat" blowjob. The pressing of the glans of the penis against the roof of the mouth and far back in the mouth in an area anatomists call the soft palate will cause a person to automatically gag. This gag instinct can be suppressed by prodigious saliva manufacture and constant swallowing.

7. True. According to years of surveys done by numerous pornographic and soft-core pornographic magazines, respondents indicate that more men are interested in going down on a woman who has been waxed or shaved. Aside from the no-hairs-in-the-mouth issue, a bare vagina sends an erotic thrill down most men's spines. With the hair gone, you can "see everything," plus a shaved pubis appears larger and more pronounced than one that is covered.

8. True. The minerals magnesium, calcium, iron, phosphorus, potassium, manganese, zinc, sodium, and copper that make asparagus so nutritionally good for you at the same time make semen taste bad. Asparagus-scented urine has a strong, unpleasant odor and asparagus-imbued semen has a rank, medicinal taste.

9. b. Watermelon, like asparagus a natural diuretic, is not only good for you in terms of minerals and vitamins, but it has the

unusual and inspired effect of making semen taste sweet. Watermelon-laced semen is sweeter, thinner, almost ambrosial. If you want your partner to lap your stuff up, try eating a big slice of watermelon an hour or two before lovemaking.

10. b. Pearl diving, canyon yodeling, box lunch—not to mention muff barking and talking to the canoe driver—are all crude synonyms for cunnilingus, or the act that can be described as tonguing a woman on the vulva and clitoris.

Positions

IT'S BEEN SAID there are over six hundred postures, positions, and poses, that can be assumed by sexual partners. The sheer volume of positions possible is a mind-boggler! Attempting to pull off all these positions, even in a lifetime of sex, requires the athletic ability of a Olympic gymnast, the flexibility of a yogi, and the stamina of a dozen mule teams. Becoming expert at yoga or Pilates surely helps! Many sexual positions can only be achieved by supremely gifted people whose minds and bodies are curious enough and limber enough to go for the gold. Some of these positions may seem freaky, although many are minor variations on very common themes.

One of the great losses to the vast realm of sexual culture is the beautiful, often fanciful names that sexual positions were given by the great ancient students of lovemaking. Back in the days when lovemaking was considered an art, great lovers were celebrated for their knowledge about something so primitive, so central to the life experience. The Arabic people as well as the Hindu and the Sanskrit cultures and the ancient Chinese invented glorious names to describe the various positions and great acts of love. What a pity so many of these wonderful names are lost now.

1. What is the history behind the missionary position? How did it get its name?
   a. Amused Polynesians, who naturally gravitated toward a squatting position for sex, so named this position after it was advocated to them by European missionaries.
   b. This is the position in which English Puritan missionaries made love and were spied on by the Native Americans.
   c. Because of religious beliefs dictating that lovemaking should only occur for the purpose of conception, sex was perceived as a mission; hence the name.
   d. Pagan savages who mixed it up sexually with the random Pilgrim so named the position as it was the only one the Pilgrims ever knew.

2. What is soixante-neuf, or "sixty-nine"?
   a. A position where each partner is able to simultaneously pleasure the other with lips, mouth, and tongue
   b. A position where one partner sucks and licks the other's toes
   c. A game where each partner races to see who can orgasm in just under 69 seconds
   d. A gang bang involving 69 participants, some of whom just take the role of voyeurs

3. The position the Chinese refer to as the "jade flute" requires the woman to be:
   a. On her hands and knees with her ankles crossed behind her
   b. On her knees with her hands on the man's buttocks and her mouth fixed tight around his cock
   c. On her back with her knees tucked around her ears
   d. Facing the man and holding his penis with her fingers on top and her thumbs underneath the shaft while her mouth gets busy

4. "The cascade" lovemaking position can be described as what?
   a. The lovers make love under a waterfall, or, failing that, running water.
   b. It's "69" position, but executed standing up.
   c. "The cascade" is a synonym for "golden showers."
   d. In a successful "cascade" the ejaculate lands in the lover's mouth.

5. When the woman lifts both her thighs in the air to meet her lover, this is called:
   a. The floating position
   b. The flying position
   c. The rising position
   d. The legs-in-the-air position

6. When the woman bends her knees into her chest to give her partner more access to her vagina, this is called:
   a. The Minotaur position
   b. The pincers position
   c. The bent position
   d. The crab position

7. When a couple assumes the lotus position, this means:
   a. The lovers' lower legs are entwined.
   b. The man is bent over the woman.
   c. The woman is crouched on top of the man.
   d. The lovers' bodies are twisted together like snakes.

8. To achieve the reversed matrimonial position, the woman should be in what posture?
    a. She should lie on him with her legs astride or between his.
    b. The woman is on top of the man, period.
    c. The man sits in a chair and the woman sits on his lap.
    d. To achieve reversed matrimonial, one must be conjoined with someone not their legal partner.

9. The flanquette position asks that the partners arrange themselves so that the woman lies facing the man with one of her legs between his and one of his legs between hers. The benefit of this position is that:
    a. Pressure is put on the bladder which may lead to a more intense orgasm.
    b. Extra clitoral pressure is achieved by the man's thigh when he presses down hard with it.
    c. Circulation is somewhat impeded in the lower extremities; at the moment of truth, the legs are released, resulting in a more intense orgasm.
    d. The sensation of leg rubbing against leg is extremely pleasurable to some partners.

10. The "X" position can be briefly described as:
    a. The person on the bottom deliberately splays his or her arms and legs.
    b. The person on top deliberately splays his or her arms and legs.
    c. One partner draws a large "X" on the other's genitals and then uses it as a bulls' eye.
    d. The woman sits astride the man while his penis is fully inserted. Then she lies back until each partner's head

and torso are between each other's wide-open thighs. They next clasp hands and coordinate slow wriggling movements that will keep them close to orgasm for a long time.

11. The French call all rear entry positions save the ones where the woman inserts one leg between her man's or is half turned on her side by what name?
    a. Croupade
    b. Engagement
    c. Le style un chien
    d. Ze back door

12. The French call any half-rear, half-side entry position by what name?
    a. Cuissade
    b. Croissant
    c. Croupier
    d. Le couche

13. A key benefit of the rear entry position for women is that:
    a. They can pretend they're having sex with somebody else.
    b. They can watch something else going on in the room, like that episode of *Law and Order* they don't want to miss.
    c. The position encourages her partner to massage and masturbate her clitoris with his fingers even as he is penetrating her with his penis.
    d. All of the above

14. Sex therapists sometimes recommend this position as a cure for partial impotence. What is it?
    a. Mutual masturbation while facing each other in the traditional yogi lotus position
    b. Head to toe
    c. Toe to head
    d. The lazy position

15. When a woman can bring her partner to orgasm solely by squeezing her vaginal muscles, this—usually but not always accomplished when the woman is on top—is called:
    a. Pouilly Fume
    b. Pouilly Fuse
    c. Piccadilly
    d. Pompoir

16. The "reverse cowgirl" position looks like this:
    a. The woman rides the man facing forward.
    b. The woman rides the man facing backward.
    c. The woman rides the man's face.
    d. The woman is ridden by the man.

17. During lovemaking, when many sexual postures are used in sequence, the goal is to move as smoothly as possible from position to position. Sex this way is said to be most like:
    a. Dancing
    b. Wrestling
    c. Rowing
    d. Bowling

18. The position where a man stands between a woman's legs and enters her from behind while she rests her elbows on the bed or floor or "walks" forward on her hands is called:

a. The vacuumer
b. The Australian crawl
c. The wheelbarrow position
d. The reformer

Answers to Positions

1. a. European missionaries, sent to Polynesia to convert the natives to Christianity denounced the natives preferred rear entry position for making love as being bestial and barbaric. Citing the importance of establishing intimacy, they insisted lovers in coitus be positioned face to face. They also advocated the female lying prone with the male in the superior position. The reinforcement of male dominance, not female pleasure, was part of the missionary position message. The missionary position today is often mocked for its somewhat puritanical name, yet it remains one of the most popular positions in the modern Western repertoire.

2. a. Soixante-neuf, or "sixty-nine," is a position that requires each partner to have his or her head above, under, or around the other partner's groin. The name derives from the way the numbers 6 and 9 are an upside-down mirror image of one another. Sixty-nine is usually performed on a bed. The partners can be of either gender. A man can perform cunnilingus on a woman while at the same time she performs fellatio on him. Two men can perform fellatio on each other and two women can eat each other out. Some couples find "69" to be too distracting. They say they can't concentrate on their own orgasm when they're busy doing someone else. When both parties enjoy it, "69" is said to be the ultimate genital kiss.

3. d. The Chinese have a lot of fancy names for what Americans lump under one heading: hand job. The jade flute is an old Asian technique, perfected by expensive prostitutes and Geishas. Essentially it is an orally enhanced hand job. The woman may or may not be clothed. What is necessary is that she sit astride the man, who is usually naked, and take his penis in two hands, her fingers on the top of the shaft and her thumbs underneath while her mouth caresses and pumps him. This combination mouth-hand position can be done on a flaccid or erect penis. In fact, it's a good way to plump a slow-rising penis up. Much of the focus in these hand techniques is in fact to encourage the man and bring him to full arousal. The hand provides an assist to the mouth and takes some of the fatigue of the oral work off the woman.

4. b. The cascade position is a standing-up oral-sex position, but both parties are not on their feet, either. The woman lies face down across the bed, her head over the edge, while the man stands astride her face and then bends over and lifts her up with her legs hung around his neck. Don't try this if you have back problems or if one of you could stand to go on a serious diet.

5. c. When a woman lifts both her thighs high in the air to meet her lover, it's called "the rising position" because it appears that the woman is "rising up" to meet the man, or, more precisely, his divine phallus.

6. d. Possibly the position where a woman bends her knees into her chest to give her partner more access to her vagina is called the crab because a woman looks crablike when she performs it.

7. a. The lotus position requires that the two lovers' legs from the knees down are entwined. The name is derived from the Kama Sutra, which labeled its classical sex positions according to tantric yogic positions and techniques.

8. a. In the reversed matrimonial position, the woman is on top of the man with her legs astride or between his.

9. b. Maximal clitoral pleasure is said to be derived from the complicated flanquette position.

10. d. The "X" position is hard to pull off, but so many people like it because it's ideal for prolonged intercourse that can last for hours.

11. a. Croupade is the name the French use to describe all rear entry positions except ones where the woman reclines on her side.

12. a. The French refer to any half-rear, half-side entry position as "Cuissade," which sounds in English a lot like cuisanart, but isn't. This is a low-impact, lazy kind of position, best for long, directionless lovemaking that takes up half an afternoon. Not recommended for slam-bam, thank-you-ma'am, hot and breathless types.

13. d. The rear entry position has a lot to recommend it. You don't have to look at your partner if you are very annoyed or angry with him or her. You don't have to look at your partner, period—very handy if you don't really know him or her. Very deep penetration can be achieved in this position, which also allows for fondling and caressing of other body parts such as the breast and the vulva. The rear entry position has stood the test of time, even if some naysayers knock it for being too bestial.

14. d. The lazy position is a favorite for many reasons, not the least of which is to boost male morale and possibly cure partial impotence. It's also a good choice for heavyset or slightly disabled people. This rear entry position asks that both partners recline on their sides. The woman draws one leg up and sticks her bottom out. It can be managed even when the man has a very limited erection or, in some cases, no erection.

15. d. When a woman can induce a man's orgasm simply by squeezing him internally, she is considered to be a very accomplished lover and one to be prized. Pompoir is just another name for "kegel," a medical technique performed by and made popular by women who have been told by their doctors to strengthen their vaginal muscles as a way to cure incontinence.

16. b. The reverse cowgirl is a female superior position where the woman sits astride the recumbent man, facing away from him. His view is of her back, her buttocks, her vagina and anus and the backs of her thighs. This position is less comfortable for deep penetration because of the angle of the vagina, but very good for the penis stimulating the clitoris.

17. a. Comparisons have long been made between good sex and good dancing. Moving smoothly and fluidly from one position to the next requires coordination and connection, whether in bed or on the dance floor. A partner who consistently steps on your feet probably will do the same thing in bed.

18. c. This ungainly position, commonly called "the wheelbarrow," is a rear entry position. In essence the woman is the wheelbarrow and the man is pushing it.

Anal Sex

W<small>HILE ONCE CONSIDERED</small> the ultimate dirty deed, anal sex is, according to the International Center for HIV/AIDS Research at the University of California, San Francisco, growing in popularity. Although anal sex was for many years considered the purview of homosexuals and desperate guys in jail, a growing number of sexually active heterosexual women engage in anal sex. Whatever your views are on the subject, make sure that if you engage in this activity, you come to the experience well prepared!

1. Anal masturbation prior to engaging in actual anal sex will help a person:
   a. Become more in tune with their anus and what feels good to them
   b. Will warm up both partners for the big show down the road
   c. Have a more intense orgasm
   d. All of the above

2. T<small>RUE OR</small> F<small>ALSE</small>. When inserting foreign objects into the anus, ensure that anything that goes in must have a flared base.

3. The main reason people feel uncomfortable with the idea of anal sex is because:
   a. Sodomy is illegal in many states.
   b. The connection between the anus and defecation is awfully close for comfort and seems anti-sexual.
   c. The Bible says anal sex is immoral and unnatural.
   d. We all learn at an early age that if something is dirty, we shouldn't put our mouths on it.

4. An impromptu protective barrier used for the purpose of safeguarding oneself and one's partner during anal-oral sex can be fashioned on the spur of the moment from which common household item?
   a. A thin latex glove
   b. A piece of plastic wrap
   c. A condom
   d. All of the above

5. What is the term many sex educators use to describe the reflexive action of the sphincter muscles when a finger, penis, or other object penetrates the anus?
   a. Winking
   b. Blinking
   c. Twinkling
   d. Nodding

6. What is the most essential element to achieving truly memorable anal sex?
   a. Trust
   b. Love
   c. One partner must be willing to subjugate him- or herself
   d. Both partners should be at least 21

7. The missionary position is one of four common positions for engaging in anal sex. Why would anyone want to have anal sex in the missionary position?
   a. The receptive partner has to do the least amount of work.
   b. The partners are facing each other, facilitating communication.
   c. Penetration is easily achieved.
   d. It gives the person on top a feeling of power.

8. When engaging in anal sex, a receptive partner who has less anal sex experience should be on top because:
   a. He or she has more control.
   b. He or she can touch, stroke, pinch or rub their own or their partner's body.
   c. He or she can stimulate another orifice more easily.
   d. All of the above.

9. TRUE OR FALSE. The doggie-style position for anal sex is more popular in pornographic movies (straight and gay) than it is in real life.

10. The primary objection to the spooning (or side-by-side position) for anal sex is that:
    a. It takes too long to achieve orgasm in this position.
    b. Unless the penetrating partner has a particularly large member, insertion may be difficult.
    c. You don't get the depth of penetration you get from some other positions.
    d. The partners should be of similar size.

11. TRUE OR FALSE. Anal fisting, which is a coitus where one person introduces their fist into another person's rectum, is an activity only practiced by gay men.

12. In the anal sex scene of Bernardo Bertolucci's 1972 epic art-house classic, *Last Tango in Paris,* what unorthodox lubricant did Marlon Brando use to ravish Maria Schneider?
   a. His own saliva
   b. A stick of butter
   c. A bar of melted chocolate
   d. Actually, he didn't use a lubricant

13. TRUE OR FALSE. Straight men who enjoy anal sex are really gay.

14. Plastic sheets found in hospital supply stores are often used by couples engaging in anal sex because anal sex is messy! The popular slang name for these sheets is:
   a. Tossaways
   b. Ass sheets
   c. Pleasure sheets
   d. Chucks

15. This clever French expression to describe the act of inserting one finger in one's partner's anus moments before orgasm is called:
   a. Petrarch
   b. Postillionage
   c. Pouilly Fume
   d. Postmaster position

16. TRUE OR FALSE. After anal sex, the receptive partner should always have an enema.

17. What well-known writer of erotica described the activity of anal fisting among lesbians?
    a. Henry Miller
    b. Susie Bright
    c. George Sands
    d. Pat Califia

18. TRUE OR FALSE. If both partners are HIV-positive, condoms are unnecessary when engaging in anal sex.

Answers to Anal Sex

1. d. Playing, toying with, kissing, stroking, and fondling the anus prior to engaging in anal intercourse will warm up both partners, help the receiving partner better understand their own physiology and level of response, heighten sensation, possibly result in a more intense orgasm, and generally make the anal sex experience more pleasurable.

2. True. When inserting any foreign object (other than a finger, a tongue, or someone's penis) into the anus, it is critical to make sure the object has a flared base. The reason? Reflex actions particular to the anus can actually suction things into it, possibly resulting in an embarrassing trip to the closest emergency room! A flared base at least ensures that you can get the object out.

3. d. There's no getting around it. It goes back to the old potty-training days. The butt is considered to be dirty. Therefore most people think you shouldn't be putting your mouth on it.

4. d. To protect both partners during oral-anal sex, protective barriers such as dental dams are recommended as a means of avoiding sexually transmitted diseases between partners. Monogamous couples may not need a protective barrier during oral-anal sex, or analingus. But for couples who aren't that close or committed, protection is essential. Even a thin latex glove, a scrap of unused kitchen plastic wrap, or even a torn-apart condom will do the job. In case you're wondering how to use the latex glove, the idea is to cut off all the fingers and leave the palm part and the thumb. The thumb part is tops for covering your tongue so you can safely orally penetrate your partner as the palm part covers the rest of the vulva.

5. a. It's an odd thing, but the sphincter muscles of the anal canal react to something being inserted into it by grasping and swallowing it up. Many sex educators call this reflex "winking." Being aware of this physiological phenomenon makes anal sex so much easier. Never poke the anus. To get it to yield, merely place the tip of the finger, the tip of a penis, or head of the dildo against the anus and gently press. Amazingly, the anus will open easily and invite the penetrating object in.

6. a. Trust is the most significant factor to keep in mind when two (or more) people are engaging in anal sex. So much about anal sex mythology is about fear. The more faith your partner has that you won't hurt him or her, the more confidence you'll inspire.

7. b. Most people consider it an enhancement when the sexual partners can see each other's faces, touch each other, and speak or nonverbally communicate. The missionary position for anal sex, which involves the receiving partner lying on their back with his or her legs extended or resting on the penetrating partner's shoulders, affords the most possibility for any and all communications, directives, or even admonitions.

8. d. Being on top, whether in an anal sex situation or a vaginal insertion, gives the partner on top maximum control, flexibility, a greater range of motion, and the opportunity to stimulate themselves or insert other objects into unused orifices.

9. True. According to porn actresses interviewed in a wide variety of adult publications, the doggie-style position for anal sex looks great on film, but in real life, most women don't find it comfortable. The position is hard to maintain for any period of time, the angle of penetration runs the risk of going too deep, there is less control for the recipient in this position, and if their face is crushed into a pillow or the bedding, they can't breathe.

10. c. While the spooning, or side-by-side, position for anal sex can be very luxurious, long lasting, and pleasant, deep penetration in this position is impossible. On the other hand, if you've got all the time in the world, go ahead and try it!

11. False. Fisting is a sex act most often associated with gay men. However, many lesbians enjoy and utilize it, as do some hetero couples, especially those who have been exposed to and find excitement in gay male pornographic literature and images. The Western culture practice of fisting, whether it be anal or vaginal, only began to be documented by sex researchers and anecdotally the 1960s during the sexual revolution. But in Indian and Chinese sexual culture, fisting has existed for thousands of years for both gays and straights.

12. b. A stick of butter is what Brando (Paul) used in the now-famous X-rated scene of *Last Tango in Paris*.

13. False. While anal sex is a very popular gay male sexual activity, the desire for it is not limited to gay men. Men who

identify as heterosexual are not repressing homosexual tendencies or desires because they want to engage in anal sex with their female partners. It's been said that gay men have more oral sex than they do anal sex, but nobody ever thinks a straight man who asks for fellatio is "really gay."

14. d. The street name for the plastic sheets used as underpads in hospitals and commonly used by practitioners of anal sex is "chucks" because after you use them and they've been heartily desecrated, you just ball them up and chuck them out!

15. b. Postillionage is a popular image in French pornography. It involves inserting or placing pressure on the anus of one's partner when one suspects that orgasm (theirs) is imminent. A small vibrator will also do the trick.

16. False. After anal sex, the receptive partner should avoid having an enema. Although the impulse to cleanse one's body of ejaculate and/or lubricant following a bout of anal sex is strong, the urge should be avoided. Why? Because anal sex, even with a lot of lubrication, causes minuscule abrasions to the delicate tissue of the rectum and the anus, and an enema will only further irritate those tissues. A bath, however, is not unwarranted. Soreness, gas, irregular bowel movements, and even slight spotting of blood are all common aftereffects of anal sex, although none of these conditions is considered dangerous.

17. d. In her collection of short stories, *Macho Sluts*, published in 1988, Pat Califia, author of *Sex Changes*, *Public Sex*, and *No Mercy* detailed the activity known as anal fisting among S&M–loving lesbians. Since the 1980's this author has educated people about sexual minority issues and has been an outspoken voice in favor of sexual freedom among consenting adults. More

recently, Pat has become Patrick, and although wheelchair bound from an autoimmune disease called fibromyalgia, is making the transition from being a female to male person.

18. False. Even if both partners know they are HIV-positive, they still should practice safer sex to avoid being exposed to different strains of the virus, or transmitting opportunistic infections and sexually transmitted diseases.

It's All How You Say It: Sexual Slang

Very few of us forget the first slang terms we heard and adopted to describe sex. By the time a person is finished with elementary school, they usually have learned all the important four-letter words! You might have even gotten your butt kicked for repeating them, even if it didn't stop you from running off your mouth. Slang words are fun and also are a record of our culture. Our values, fears, hatreds, and errors are all embodied in slang terminology and euphemism, especially when the words are provocative and prohibited. Richard A. Spears, an internationally renowned slang expert, says slang was originally the patter of criminals, unwelcome in polite company. Either in spite of its unsavory roots—or because of them—sex slang is always popular, and the words themselves are constantly in flux. New slang, like "camel's toe," could never have come about before the age of spandex. In this section, you will be tested on your scatological knowledge, and you may learn some new vocabulary and fill in some blanks in your verbal repertoire!

1. To rim someone means to:
   a. Have anal intercourse with them
   b. Perform oral sex on a vagina
   c. Perform analingus on them
   d. Use a kind of vibrator on them

2. In sexual slang, a "bag" refers to what?
   a. An udder
   b. A douche
   c. A scrotum
   d. All of the above

3. The following expression does *not* mean "to masturbate":
   a. Beat the bishop
   b. Beat pounder
   c. Beat the dummy
   d. Beat off

4. A glory hole is:
   a. A vagina
   b. A rectum
   c. A hole in a stall partition in a men's public restroom, used for fellatio purposes or to allow one man to sneak looks at other men's penises
   d. A prostitute

5. The expression "man in the boat" refers to:
   a. Nipples which have become aroused and engorged
   b. The clitoris
   c. A very wet vagina
   d. The glans, or head, of the penis

6. To say someone is "cocked up" is to say:
   a. They've been impregnated.
   b. They were rendered intoxicated before being seduced.
   c. They are a whoremonger or notorious fornicator.
   d. They exhibit nymphomania type behavior.

7. In gay parlance, a bronco is:
   a. The top man
   b. A young male who is difficult to restrain during intercourse
   c. A wildly enthusiastic sexual person
   d. A partner who has sex like a horse

8. Which phrase is *not* slang terminology for the sex act known as cunnilingus:
   a. Larking
   b. Muff diving
   c. Skull job
   d. Cunny burrow

9. The slang words "buck face," "cornuto," "horn grower," "ramhead," and "green goose" all refer to what?
   a. A horny but recently virginal man who has sex with his fiancée before marriage
   b. Someone who has committed adultery
   c. A cuckold, or a man whose wife is known to have cheated on him
   d. A horny but virginal man

10. The expression "full house" has what particular meaning?
    a. One is engaging in sex with more than one partner at one time.
    b. One has all their orifices—anus, vagina, mouth—engaged in a sex act simultaneously during any one sexual session.
    c. One has more than one venereal disease at the same time.
    d. One is pregnant.

11. To "trim the buff" means to:
    a. Trim the pubic hair region
    b. Break in a virgin
    c. Have sex with a woman who has shaved or otherwise defoliated her pubic region
    d. Have sex with a well-built homosexual man

12. What is "camel's toe"?
    a. A position mentioned in the *Kama Sutra*
    b. A situation where a woman's pants or underwear creep up into the cleft of her vagina
    c. An ancient tool for making love
    d. A bestial sexual act

13. Hoovering, piston jobs, French tricks, and smoke are all slang words referring to what kind of sexual activity?
    a. Cunnilingus
    b. Anal sex
    c. Fellatio
    d. Group sex

14. The portion of the body sometimes referred to as "the taint" is what part?
    a. The vagina
    b. The rectum
    c. The perineum
    d. The head of the penis

15. A pearl diver is an individual who:
    a. Performs oral sex on a penis
    b. Performs cunnilingus while focusing their attention almost exclusively on the clitoris
    c. Seeks to break in virgins and introduce them to the joys of sexual pleasure
    d. Is an impotent man who can only perform oral sex on a woman

16. To snog or snoggle someone means to:
    a. Have intercourse with them
    b. Cuddle and kiss and caress them
    c. Ejaculate on them
    d. Spoon with them

17. A "snapper" is:
    a. A tight vagina
    b. A penis
    c. A popper, or ampule of amyl nitrite, especially enjoyed by gay men while having sex
    d. All of the above

18. What is the meaning of "Capistrano"?
    a. The pet name for a popular brand of vibrator
    b. To have sex with someone while they are incarcerated
    c. To offer and perform on someone oral sex
    d. To have sex with someone in a moving vehicle

19. What exactly is "a pearl necklace"?
    a. A piece of jewelry bestowed by a smitten and pearl-loving admirer
    b. Love bites or hickeys that encircle the beloved's neck
    c. Droplets of semen that form a "necklace" around someone's neck following an act of fellatio that does not result in swallowing
    d. Any ejaculate deposited outside of the body

20. If you're felching someone, what are you doing to them?
    a. You're licking their anus.
    b. You're licking their feet.
    c. You're sucking their penis.
    d. You've nose-dived into their vagina.

21. What does "snowballing" mean?
    a. Having sex with multiple women in one night
    b. Having the guy's semen spit back into his mouth
    c. Having sex in the snow
    d. Going without sex for a prolonged period

22. The expression "Riding St. George" is a sexual euphemism meaning what?
    a. The woman is on her hands and knees.
    b. The woman is wearing an S&M piece of equipment resembling a saddle.

    c. The woman is astride a man who is reclining on his back.

    d. One woman rides the man's face while another woman rides his penis.

23. To refer to someone's Johnson is to refer to their what?
    a. Penis
    b. Anus
    c. Fist and their forearm, as in the sexual activity of fisting
    d. Mug, or face

24. What does the slang term "teabagging" mean?
    a. Using iced tea as a body rub and aphrodisiac stimulant
    b. An oral sex technique where the testicles of one partner are draped like a pair of teabags over the nose of the other partner while that partner performs fellatio on him
    c. Moistened tea bags are inserted into the vagina after sex to cleanse it
    d. A sex act involving hot water and dipping a body part into it

25. Other than tits, boobs, ninnies, headlights, and chi-chis, what is another slang term to describe a woman's breasts?
    a. Jits
    b. Bracks
    c. Rack
    d. Brim

Answers to It's All How You Say It: Sexual Slang

1. c. Rimming, which is a slang term that originated in the United States sometime in the early 1900s, specifically refers to the sexual activity of applying one's tongue to another's anal orifice. While once believed to be a homosexual act, the practice of rimming has become more widespread and is not limited to male-on-male action. A rimadonna, on the other hand, is always a homosexual male who prefers to perform or receive analingus instead of engaging in alternative kinds of sex.

2. d. An udder, a douche, and a scrotum can all be referred to as "bags," a singularly offensive colloquial expression that seems to have sprung into the popular vernacular in Britain around 1500 and has endured ever since. The word "bag" has also been used to describe old women, prostitutes of a certain age, contraceptive diaphragms, a condom, and the female genitals. The 1960s American expression "What's your bag?" has an entirely different meaning.

3. b. Although the lewd expressions "beat the bishop," "beat the dummy," and "beat off" are all synonymous with masturbation, a "beat pounder" is another term for police officer. The expression "beating the gun," incidentally, does not indicate that one is masturbating oneself or masturbating a police officer, but rather that one is having sex with one's intended spouse before the marriage has been made official.

4. c. While it is true that a glory hole is also another commonly used term for a British military dugout, its more sexually oriented and certainly contemporary definition is a small hole made in the privacy partitions of male public restrooms contrived for the sole purpose of illicit homosexual acts. While sex

in public places is officially against the law, the glorious glory hole provides the ultimate way to deliciously and anonymously connect with another person.

5. b. Since the 17th century, the portion of the female anatomy officially and medically known as the clitoris has been dubbed by clever linguists "the man in the boat." Other slang for this elusive and sometimes hard-to-locate portion of the female anatomy includes the clitty, the button, and the boy in the boat.

6. a. Cocked up is British farmer slang for getting someone pregnant. Other colorful vernacular expressions to describe this condition might be to say someone has been storked or that they are "up a pole."

7. b. In gay vernacular, rich with its own particularly descriptive and lewd slang, a young male who is a real handful, and who perhaps requires restraint while one is actively engaged in sex with him, is popularly known (and probably praised for this quality) as a bronco.

8. d. There are many slang expressions for the sex act known as cunnilingus, too many to list here. Larking, muff diving, skull job, talk to the canoe driver, eat out, box lunch . . . the list is endless. Cunny burrow, on the other hand, merely refers to the female genitals, probably because a vagina resembles in some fashion a bunny burrow or rabbit hole.

9. c. A man whose wife has committed adultery is known as a cuckold, an expression that dates back possibly to the Middle Ages. Certainly Chaucer used the expression. A man whose wife has betrayed him with another man can also be known as a cornuto, a buck face, a horn grower, and a green goose. He usually also can be described as being extremely angry.

10. c. The expression "full house," sexy and seductive as the phrase may sound to the ears, in gay slang means a plethora of bad news—that an individual has contracted and is capable of passing on to others more than one venereal disease at one time.

11. b. Trimming the buff is a slang term for terminating a female's virginity or otherwise rupturing her hymen. Other slang words for spoiling a woman's virginity are "pick her cherry," "crack her pitcher," "cop a bean," and just plain "trim." The word "trim" itself is slang for vagina, particularly a young, inexperienced vagina.

12. b. A camel's toe is basically a female "wedgie" involving the pudenda, not the asscrack. You've seen it. It's the situation where a female's trousers, bathing suit, or panties are so tight and close-fitting they become wedged into the cleft of her vagina, creating a split-hoof effect, much like that of a camel's toe. Check it out next time you're thumbing through *National Geographic*. Some naughty girls deliberately wear their pants this tight to show off their clefts. Leotards and gymnasts' suits often inadvertently reveal the camel toe situation, another reason to attend gymnastic meets.

13. c. The use of the tongue or lips to stimulate the penis is referred to by any number of colorful expressions, including hoovering, piston jobs, French tricks, and smoking. The expressions munching, pipe job, knob jobs, and blow jobs are interesting substitutions.

14. c. The perineum of either the male or female body is sometimes called "the taint," an expression that dates back to the early 1600s. The perineum is the region of the body located between the anus and the scrotum in the male, and between the

anus and the vagina or vulva in the female. The word "taint" is said to be a conjunction of the ancient words "tis" and "ain't" because the area "tisn't arse" and it "ain't pussy," which, logically, makes it "the taint."

15. a. The gay slang for a person who enjoys giving another male oral pleasure is pearl diver. It is unclear where or how this term originated, but it is commonly used among homosexual males.

16. b. To snog or snoggle with someone means to cuddle, kiss, and caress them. Also known as "firkytoodling," this British slang expression has made its way into the United States vernacular, largely due to the popularity of British import novels turned into movies, with *Bridget Jones's Diary* being a primary example.

17. d. A tight vagina, a penis, and an inhalant drug are all snappers. The penis reference comes from 200-year-old British slang. The vaginal reference is strictly mid-19th-century American. The term became part of the American drug culture in the mid-20th century when street drug culture merged with existing sexual slang, and poppers or snappers became integral to the gay club scene.

18. c. Capistrano is a slang term for oral sex, although usually limited to a woman performing oral sex on a man. The origin of the phrase is believed to be a reference to March 19, St. Joseph's Day, which is when the swallows are said to return to the town of Capistrano, located in California.

19. c. A pearl necklace is a pretty term for the droplets of semen that land on a person's face and neck following a fellatio experience that does not wind up with the individual doing the fellating actually swallowing.

20. a. To felch someone means to apply the tongue to the anus. This can be a hetero- or homosexual act. This may involve licking, sucking, tickling, teasing, or otherwise tongue-torturing the anus. The tongue may actually enter the body and lightly explore inside. Felching, an act particular to anal sex but not involving the penis, is for some an extremely lewd and vulgar activity, while others consider it the consummate delight. Depending on your point of view, felching is either sublime or ridiculous . . . or just downright disgusting.

21. b. Snowballing is the act of spitting a guy's semen back into his mouth after fellatio. The guy orgasms into the girl's mouth; she kisses him and spits it back into his mouth. The act is specifically mentioned in the movie *Clerks*, directed by Kevin Smith.

22. c. The charming euphemism "Riding St. George" refers to a female superior position, meaning that the woman is astride a man who is reclining on his back. The phrase is some reference to "the dragon upon St. George," a heroic Catholic legend having to do with a maiden and her girdle and a beast led around by his neck.

23. a. A Johnson is a penis, so named after Dr. Johnson, a possibly mythological doctor of sex and, much later, sexual paraphernalia. Another personification of the penis is calling it a John Willie, which is sometimes diminished or nicknamed a Willie. There is also a John Thomas (think *Lady Chatterley's Lover*). Sailors and soldiers have often referred to their penises as Johnsons, although the phrase is now so common as to be understood by even schoolchildren.

24. b. "Teabagging," which used to be an exclusively gay term, is now general sex slang to describe an act where one partner is being fellated. The teabagging position is achieved by one person crouching in a squatting position over the face of the other person, who is reclining on his or her back. The crouching person hangs their testicles over the partner's nose and gently bounces up and down as though they were dipping teabags. When heterosexuals engage in teabagging, the woman is the one on her back and the man is the one crouched over her. It was debated on the Howard Stern show whether or not teabagging also involved the woman licking or sucking the testicles, or if the testicles are just left unlicked but dangling.

25. c. Rack is an expression commonly used to describe a woman's breasts, particularly a woman whose breasts are on the large side. Possibly in reference to "the big rack," or antlers, on a male deer, trophy hunters of women often hope to snag one with a substantial rack of breast flesh. For the record, jits is a derogatory racial term; to brack is to make a vomiting sound; and a brim is British slang for a lewd and furious woman.

Sexual Health

Sexual health, you groan. Is this going to be like the final exam in high school health class? Is this going to be the part of the quiz where you embarrassingly get every question wrong?

Without a doubt, sexual health is one of the more difficult portions of the quiz. It's amazing what we don't know (or don't want to know!) about our own sexuality! And yet it is so important, especially in this age of disease—although sexual diseases (and dysfunction) are actually nothing new. Sexually transmitted diseases, not to mention bad sexual mental health, have been around since time immemorial. In fact, before penicillin, people used to die from them, even if their demises took a very long time.

Before you expire from anxiety about how much or little you know, just remember, the point of this quiz is not just to test your knowledge, but to encourage your enlightenment. Absorb all the new information you can, and incorporate it into your own sex life! This section of the quiz includes information on the reproductive organs, contraception and sexually transmitted diseases, and sex-related mental health disorders. Consider yourself to be very educated and talented if you know all the answers on these topics!

The Reproductive Organs

Fallopian tubes, uteri, ovaries, testes, and scrotums may not be the most glamorous parts of the body. It's hard to be glamorous when you can't easily be seen! Nevertheless, these essential bits and pieces are necessary components to the continuance of the human species—at least until they perfect cloning, that is!

1. The ovaries are female reproductive organs that come in pairs, each one located on either side of the uterus, which is the female organ designed to carry and partially nourish a fetus. What part of the female anatomy connects the ovaries to each other?
   a. The vestibule
   b. The Bartholin's gland
   c. The fallopian tubes
   d. The labia minora

2. A woman's ovaries can be compared in size to what fruit or vegetable?
   a. An almond
   b. Plum tomatoes
   c. A head of garlic
   d. Mandarin oranges

3. The word "testicle," has something in common with the word "testament." Other than the obvious "sounds like. . . ," what is it the two words share in common?
   a. The word "testicle" can be found in the Bible.
   b. The word "testicle" comes from the Latin word, "testis," which means "witness."
   c. The word "testicle" was first pronounced by one of the guests at the Last Supper.

d. The word "testicle" has nothing in common with the word "testament."

4. While the presence of testosterone in a male is very good, too much testosterone can cause which of the following problems?
   a. Unsightly hair sprouting from the back and shoulders
   b. Acne
   c. Constant, unwanted erections
   d. Baldness, growth of the prostate, possibly prostate cancer

5. TRUE OR FALSE. A man with a lot of testosterone is a man with a lot of lust.

6. A healthy male produces sperm all day long. In fact, he's a virtual sperm factory. In the body of a healthy male, the factory never really shuts down. While production rates might be voluminous, one cc of sperm contains approximately how many sperm cells?
   a. 2 million
   b. 10 million
   c. 40 million
   d. 100 million

7. What is the most unusual side effect associated with the prescription drug Viagra?
   a. Night sweats
   b. Hallucinations that one is a sexual Superman
   c. A slight memory loss, as in who was it exactly sharing the bed
   d. Mild and temporary visual changes, including color perception changes, light perception changes, and blurred vision

8. In the great search for a "female Viagra" (and so far the perfect one hasn't been found), only one product received FDA approval. What is that product?
   a. Because
   b. At Last
   c. Finally
   d. Aware

9. What popular antidepressant, stop-smoking prescription drug is the only one proven to not affect sexual function?
   a. Wellbutrin
   b. Prozac
   c. Zoloft
   d. Xanax

10. What are the Bartholin's glands?
   a. A network of nerve-rich material located and surrounding the vagina and the anus that supports the pelvic cavity
   b. Two erectile folds of skin between the labia majora
   c. An erectile hooded organ at the upper joining of the labia
   d. Two small round structures, one on each side of the vaginal opening

11. The scrotal pouch is divided into two smaller pouches, each containing one testicle with its epididymis. What is the epididymis?
   a. The epididymis is the gelatinous fluid that surrounds each teste.
   b. The epididymis is the tubing that carries sperm out of the testes.
   c. The epididymis is connected to the testicle and overlies it like a cap.
   d. The epididymis is made of collagen.

Answers to The Reproductive Organs

1. c. The fallopian tubes are an essential part of the female reproductive tract. Long slender tubes, their job is to be the connector and passageway from which eggs pass from the ovaries into the uterus.

2. a. The ovaries, upon which so much depends, are actually very small in size. Under normal conditions, they should be about the same size as an almond. Women undergoing fertility treatments may hear their doctor say their ovaries have grown to the "size of grapefruit." This is considered good, not a cause for worry. Gonal-F and other ovulation medications spur the formation of multiple follicles in the ovaries, a positive thing if one is going to extraordinary methods to conceive.

3. b. In Latin, "testis" also means "witness." In the great olden days of Rome, a person missing his testicles (a eunuch) was definitely not considered a man and therefore could not testify in a court of law.

4. d. Testosterone is fabulous, but a manly man can have too much of a good thing. An overabundance of testosterone can cause a number of male problems, including baldness, growth of the prostate, and, eek, prostate cancer.

5. False. The level of testosterone changes from day to day in every man and from one man to another. Elevated testosterone levels do not have any effect on lusty feelings or make for a bigger penis. Sex hormones are only needed in small quantities by the body, and testosterone is no exception. But even if a guy only has one ball, it produces enough testosterone to make everything work the way Nature intended.

6. c. One cc of sperm contains 40 million sperm cells. But that doesn't mean everything produced can be called premium. About half the amount of sperm cells produced by the male body actually don't work very well, either because they didn't come off the assembly line right or because when called into action, they don't always perform. Mother Nature favors quantity over quality, and that's why she makes so much. Yet it only takes one sperm cell to fertilize a female egg.

7. d. Mild and thankfully temporary visual changes, including changes in color perception, light perception, and blurred vision are some of the unusual side effects reported by Viagra users. Sounds almost like a psychedelic acid trip. Seems like a small price to pay (and possibly a real enhancement) in exchange for a super erection.

8. c. A product called Finally is to date the only FDA-compliant orgasm enhancer designed exclusively for women. Supposedly it works by increasing blood flow to the genital area. The product is a cream, not a pill; it is sold over the counter, not by prescription; and it can be applied five to seven minutes before its intended use (as opposed to an hour, which is how long Viagra takes to work). It lasts for up to forty-five minutes before it should be reapplied. By contrast Viagra works for four hours, which, in some people's opinion, is an awfully long period of time.

9. a. Wellbutrin is the only known prescription antidepressant, stop-smoking drug that has been clinically proven not to affect sexual function. While other antidepressants do chemically work to improve the patient's outlook and state of mind, they often are a cause for penile dysfunction and/or loss of libido in both men and women. But not Wellbutrin, a fact the drug's manufacturer has understandably crowed about.

10. d. The Bartholin's glands are the two small, round structures that can be found on either side of the vaginal opening. The purpose of these glands is to secrete a mucuslike fluid during sexual arousal for the purpose of lubrication. In other words, it's the Bartholin's glands that make a woman wet.

11. c. The epididymis is tissue that is connected to the testicle and overlies it like a cap. It contains a substantial number of microscopically small tubes. It is from the epididymis that the vas deferens conducts freshly made sperm cells to the area of the prostate. The vas deferens runs together with blood vessels to supply blood to and from the testicle and some muscle fibers. You might describe the vas deferens as a long, thin sausage perforating the abdominal wall at the groin.

Contraception

How not to make a baby is as important a concept as how to. Contraception has always been an inflammatory subject because certain religions, for example, Roman Catholicism, have prohibitions against it. Nevertheless, the inventiveness of the human mind has led to some startling innovations and experiments to prevent pregnancy over the centuries. You might be surprised to learn just how innovative certain contraceptive methods are, even if you dare not attempt some of them!

1. One of the earliest references to birth control comes from the Bible, from the book of Genesis, which urged men to practice _____, commonly referred to as "the withdrawal method."
   a. Cunnilingus
   b. Fellatio
   c. Coitus interruptus
   d. Vicesimus sextus

2. Which ancient Roman writer counseled abstinence as a form of birth control?
   a. Virgil
   b. Pliny
   c. Homer
   d. Seneca

3. What individual or individuals have been widely perceived to be the leader of the modern contraceptive movement, and in what year?
   a. Aletta Jacobs in 1878
   b. Maria Stopes in 1921
   c. Margaret Sanger in 1916
   d. All of the above

4. Spermicide must be applied _____ and _____ the rim of the diaphragm before being inserted.
   a. Up (and) down
   b. Inside (and) around
   c. In one place (and) in the dent of the crown of
   d. To the entire diaphragm (and) with jelly to ensure the best results

5. What is the most common diaphragm size?
   a. 12 mm diameter
   b. 75 mm diameter
   c. 55 mm diameter
   d. 100 mm diameter

6. What birth control device is not recommended if a woman has more than one partner?
   a. The contraceptive sponge
   b. The cervical cap

c. The IUD

d. A condom

7. What was the contraceptive device "Elaine" on Seinfeld hoarded when she heard it was about to be taken off the market?

a. Myself

b. Vagi-Guard

c. Monistat

d. Today Sponge

8. TRUE OR FALSE. Wilt Chamberlain had his condoms custom-made.

9. Who was the inventor of the technology that made it possible to vulcanize rubber and put it to use in the manufacture of condoms, douching syringes, and "womb veils" (an early form of the diaphragm)?

a. William Seward

b. Alexander Graham Bell

c. Robert Fulton

d. Charles Goodyear

10. Which brand of condom for years carried the image of legendary lover Rudolph Valentino on its box?

a. Trojans

b. Sheik

c. Ramses

d. No brand was ever associated with Rudolph Valentino.

11. What is the name of the condom designed as a barrier con-
    traception for females?
    a. There is no female condom
    b. Summer's Eve
    c. My Way
    d. The Reality condom

12. In what year did the Roman Catholic Church make its
    first authoritative statement on birth control?
    a. 1940
    b. 1929
    c. 1900
    d. 1930

13. Out of every 100 women who use the Pill, how many will
    become pregnant during the first year of typical use?
    a. Four
    b. Five
    c. Three
    d. Ten

14. Flavored condoms were invented for what purpose?
    a. The enhancement of protected oral sex
    b. To satisfy deep sugar cravings on the part of one's partner
    c. Because condoms have been around for so many years
       manufacturers had to come up with some new stunts
    d. Flavored condoms provide an additional spermicidal
       barrier

15. The first contraceptive intrauterine device or IUD was really:
    a. An apricot pit
    b. A marble
    c. A pebble
    d. A wire clothes hanger

16. What was the great lover Casanova's contribution to contraception?
    a. He invented the first condom.
    b. He was the first to write about *coitus interruptus*.
    c. He used a lemon wedge shoved up into the vaginal canal.
    d. Casanova made no contribution to birth control.

17. Condoms not made of latex, but from the intestines of sheep, are sometimes called:
    a. Hides
    b. Lambskins
    c. Skulls
    d. Baa–Bags

18. What is the part of the male anatomy that gets snipped to complete the medical contraceptive procedure known as vasectomy?
    a. The scrotum
    b. The vas deferens
    c. The testicles
    d. The foreskin

Answers to Contraception

1. c. *Coitus interruptus* is probably the most common birth control method attempted by human beings from time immemorial. Anecdotally known as "pulling out" or "the withdrawal method," *coitus interruptus* is said to work because it theoretically prevents the semen from entering the body. However, it is an unreliable and unpredictable form of birth control because some seed usually is present at the top of the penis even before one pulls out, and partly because it's so hard to pull out when one's instinct is to plunge in. Men who perform in porn films are always expert at *coitus interruptus*, and not because they do it to prevent conception. They pull out to create "the money shot," or visible proof of semen, a necessary element in nearly all adult film. The Old Testament refers specifically to Onan in the book of Moses, who had to die because he spilled (and wasted) his seed.

2. b. Pliny the Elder, author of *Natural History*, writing between 23 and 79 A.D., counseled his readers to refrain from sex to avoid pregnancy. Heavily into the medicinal uses of marine animals and charms, farmer and gardening buff Pliny saw the hazardous results of unchecked mating and breeding, no doubt leading him to express his learned opinions on the subject of birth control.

3. d. Aletta Jacobs, Maria Stopes, and Margaret Sanger all had a considerable influence on the modern contraceptive movement, although they lived in different places and did their work at different times. Aletta Jacobs opened the first birth control clinic dispensing contraceptives and offering women internal exams in Amsterdam in 1878, and Maria Stopes did the same in London in 1921. British writer Thomas Robert Malthus had been stirring up interest in the promotion of contraception even

before the turn of the century. In 1916 Margaret H. Sanger opened the first family planning clinic in Brooklyn, New York, and was promptly arrested by the police. She served thirty days in the workhouse for "maintaining a public nuisance," but publicity and legal difficulties only raised awareness and public sympathy for her work. Sanger founded the American Birth Control League, and in 1927 organized the first World Population Conference in Geneva, Switzerland. In 1921 she became the founder of the American Birth Control League, a precursor to the International Planned Parenthood Federation.

4. b. Spermicide, whether flavored, colored, or blandly neutral, should be applied (generously) both inside and around the rim of the diaphragm prior to insertion. Spermicides intended for use with diaphragms are meant to be used with diaphragms; without the device, their efficacy is compromised. With every repeated act of intercourse, more spermicide should be applied. Some doctors recommend removing the entire diaphragm for a thorough fresh recoating before engaging in more intercourse, while others say it's fine to leave the diaphragm in place indefinitely. A correct anointing before the device goes in is essential. Careless daubing of spermicide either on top of or under or smack in the middle of a diaphragm only increases the chances of it not working well. No matter how much sex a woman is having, any diaphragm left in for several days will emit a rank odor.

5. b. The most common diaphragm size is 75 mm diameter. The range goes from 50 mm diameter to 105 mm diameters. A woman's diaphragm size, however, is subject to change. Having a baby will alter it, as will significant weight gain or loss. A woman relying on a diaphragm should have her size checked every year by her gynecologist. And she should check her diaphragm for tears or pinholes every time she uses it.

6. c. IUDs, or intrauterine device contraceptives, come in two varieties, the standard Paragard IUD and the Copper T Progestasert. An IUD must be inserted by a doctor. Because of the strings that hang down outside the uterus necessary to recapture them for their eventual removal, IUDs are not recommended for women who have more than one partner because of the string's propensity for transmitting sexual disease. The strings do not seem to pose much of a problem in couples who are monogamous. IUDs should also be eschewed by women who have one partner but whose partner has more than one partner. Is this contraceptive too confusing? Use another method.

7. d. Between 1984 and 1995, the Today Sponge was the most popular nonprescriptive contraceptive. Used by 6.4 million women, when Whitehall-Robbins stopped manufacturing the little pink piece of foam because of a problem with distribution, devoted users lost their heads. Rumors of hoarding and panic spread everywhere, so much so that the Today Sponge became the focus of a Seinfeld episode. The sponge is in the process of making its USA comeback, thanks to Allendale Pharmaceuticals in New Jersey. The sponge is readily available in Canada.

8. True. "Wilt the Stilt" told Howard Stern during an interview that he had his condoms custom-made for him. Wilt did not fit into any over-the-counter products, and since he was reputed to have enjoyed sex with literally thousands of females, the man went through a lot of them.

9. d. Although his name is forever linked with rubber, Charles Goodyear was an unsuccessful hardware salesman until business failure propelled him into the discovery of how to prevent rubber from melting. In 1839, Goodyear accidentally came upon the process for vulcanizing rubber, but failed to foresee its potential application. Unlike raw rubber, the process produced a rubber

that wasn't sticky, yet resisted freezing or softening. Durable, and resistant to abrasion as well as to gasoline, vulcanized rubber proved an excellent insulator against heat and electricity, making it as ideal a product for birth control as it was to the tire industry.

10. b. For many years the Sheik brand of condoms had Valentino's silhouette on its box cover. Although touted for his sexy silent screen roles in *A Married Virgin* (1918), *The Sheik* (1921) and *A Sainted Devil* (1924), Valentino, whose real name was Rudolfo Guglielmi, was kind of a washout in bed. His several wives and girlfriends said he was "more like a brother," which is not exactly a great recommendation.

11. d. There is only one condom made specifically for women and that is the Reality condom. This condom is a female barrier method of birth control, very popular in portions of Africa. The Reality condom is made of polyurethane as opposed to latex. The Reality female condom was approved for use in the U.S. in 1992 for vaginal contraceptive use and lauded for its impermeability to viruses. In laboratory testing it also proved less likely to tear than its latex cousins. Other possible fans of the polyurethane condom are men (and women) who suffer from latex allergies.

12. d. It was Christmas Eve, December 31, 1930, when Pope Pius XI issued an encyclical titled *Casti Canubi* (Of Chaste Marriage), denouncing artificial methods of birth control as sin. Six years later, in 1936, a devout Catholic doctor named John Rock opened a rhythm method clinic in Boston, the first of its kind in the United States. The rhythm method depends on a woman keeping exact track of her menstrual cycle and her awareness of when she is ovulating. The rhythm method is the only approved method of conception avoidance practiced by Catholics.

13. b. According to medical researchers, the Pill is considered to be one of the most effective contraceptives available today. Yet the perfect oral contraceptive is but a dream. Five out of every one hundred women taking the Pill will become pregnant during "typical use." If typical use means occasionally forgetting to take one's pill, that explains the failure rate. Side effects from the Pill include weight gain, moodiness, and breast tenderness. The Pill is not recommended for women who smoke or for some women who have a history of heart disease.

14. a. Flavored condoms, which come in tastes as diverse as banana, cherry, and chocolate (one company, Trustex, has them available in chocolate, strawberry, banana, vanilla, grape, cola, and mint) are popular for the enhancement of protected oral sex.

15. a. It's been said that contraceptive IUDs were first used by the Middle Eastern and North African tribes known as Bedouins as they traveled across the desert with their camels. Some enterprising camel owner discovered that the pit of an apricot inserted into the camel's vagina and pushed deep into her womb would interfere with pregnancy. The same principle applies today as modern docs insert intrauterine devices into women's uteruses to avoid pregnancy. To this day no one knows exactly how the IUD works. It is thought that the presence of a foreign object in the womb discourages a fertilized egg from adhering to the lining of the uterus.

16. c. Casanova, the famous lover who lived between 1725 and 1798, was an early advocate of the contraceptive lemon wedge. Sex historians believe the lemon wedge was first used during the Medieval period as a primitive, albeit fairly effective, form of birth control. Casanova gets the credit—realizing that a lemon wedge shoved up the vaginal canal and positioned against

the cervix worked to block the entrance of sperm into the female body. The citric acid naturally present in lemon also has a deleterious effect on the motility of sperm.

17. b. Although early condoms were most certainly derived from barnyard intestinal membrane, ever since the age of latex, condoms made from animal membrane, while sold and crowed about by their finicky and esoteric users, have been under the gun. In the late '80s the FDA considered putting warning labels on lambskin condoms because of questions about their efficacy. Recalls of such condoms were frequent. Today, natural lamb membrane condoms with an exclusive and trademarked Kling-Tite band are manufactured and sold by Trojan, one of the most trusted names in male contraceptives.

18. b. The vas deferens are the tubes in the testicles that when snipped, keep sperm out of the fluid that spurts from the penis during sex, causing a man to be sterile. Sperm are the reproductive cells in men, and pregnancy can occur when sperm connects with a woman's egg. Vasectomy blocks the vas deferens and keeps sperm out of the seminal fluid.

Sexual Diseases and Disorders

Not to be a bummer, but there are some downsides to sex. Sex is so much fun, but it can really make you sick. Too much sex or sex under unsafe conditions can make you feel run down, feverish, and flu-like, or it can give you nasty sores, or cause you to behave in an irresponsible manner. In the worst-case scenarios, sex might even kill you! Over the centuries, so much sickness has been associated with sex that sex has gotten a bad rap. This portion of the quiz is not meant in any way to be comprehensive of the dark encyclopedia of sexual disorders and illnesses, but a testing of your basic knowledge about sexually transmitted illnesses and clinically recognized sexual disorders.

1. What is the quick test that can be done in a doctor's office for the detection of gonorrhea?
   a. A urine test
   b. An examination of the person's throat, rectum, or genitals
   c. The Gram stain
   d. The Pap smear

2. Syphilis, and a 15th-century disease called yaws have something unique in common. What is that?
   a. Both diseases are caused by the same spirochete.
   b. They both cause their victims to have withered limbs.
   c. Both diseases can be passed by mouth.
   d. They mostly infected young people.

3. What is the medically correct name for the sexually transmitted disease also known as "the clap"?
   a. Syphilis
   b. Gonorrhea
   c. Chlamydia
   d. PID

4. Impotence is:
   a. A male erectile disorder
   b. A glandular disease
   c. A form of herpes
   d. Always associated with hair loss

5. What legislative act was passed in 1864 to protect soldiers and sailors in military and naval towns from women carrying venereal disease?
   a. The Soldiers & Sailors Act
   b. The Contagious Diseases Act
   c. The Douglas Order
   d. The Alien Registration Act

6. A person who desires to be beaten, bound, stepped on, blindfolded, whipped, electrically shocked, or flagellated for sexual purposes is called what?
   a. A tribadist
   b. A sexual masochist
   c. An auto-coprophagist
   d. A necrophiliac

7. What is Kempf's disease?
   a. A desire to copulate with animals
   b. A medical condition resulting from lack of sex
   c. An overwhelming desire to remove one's clothing in public places
   d. Homosexual panic

8. What venereal disease had the dubious distinction of being the most trendy sexually transmitted designer disease of the '80s?
   a. Chlamydia
   b. Scabies
   c. Herpes
   d. Crabs

9. What sexually transmitted virus affects the skin of the genital area and causes wartlike growths or abnormal skin changes?
   a. Scabies
   b. Vaginitis
   c. Herpes
   d. Human papillomavirus (HPV)

10. What is the biggest danger attached to the sexually transmitted disease chlamydia?
    a. Once you have it you'll never get rid of it.
    b. It scars a woman's fallopian tubes and she may not be able to become pregnant.
    c. The antibiotics you have to take to get rid of it will make you get fat.
    d. You can have it a long time and not be aware of it.

11. What disease is sometimes called "the kissing disease"?
    a. Gardnerella
    b. Mononucleosis
    c. Monilia
    d. Chancroids

12. Autoeroticism is:
    a. Making love in cars
    b. Sensual self-gratification
    c. Group sex
    d. A highly possessive form of jealousy

13. Recurrent sexual urges and sexually arousing fantasies involving nonhumans, children, or other nonconsenting

persons, or the arousal caused by humiliating oneself or somebody else is a psychiatric disease or disorder known under the general heading of:

a. Homophilia
b. Klismaphilia
c. Paraphilia
d. Polyphagia

14. What is frotteurism?

a. Intense sexual urges involving a need to put one's tongue in another person's mouth
b. A compulsion to pass sexually transmitted diseases to other people
c. Intense sexual urges involving a need to touch and rub against an unaware or nonconsenting person
d. A compulsion to use blindfolds during sex

15. A doctor may pronounce a woman frigid if she says she has which of the following characteristics?

a. The woman has no interest or desire for sex.
b. The woman appears to be a cold, withholding person.
c. The woman refuses to have sex with her regular partner on demand.
d. The woman hasn't had sex in many years.

16. Someone who is sexually aroused by the sight, sounds, smells, or tastes of human excrement is called what?

a. A somatic delusional
b. A victim of Cotard's syndrome
c. A coprophiliac
d. Codependent

17. Who wrote the breakthrough book on the people and politics of the AIDS epidemic?
    a. Primo Levi
    b. Randy Shilts
    c. David Schwartz
    d. Stewart O'Nan

18. What Hollywood movie star brought the word "AIDS" into every American household?
    a. Anthony Quinn
    b. Tony Randall
    c. Rock Hudson
    d. Claude Raines

19. TRUE OR FALSE. Anal and genital warts can recur even after they have been removed by a doctor either by applying a chemical acid or burning off with an electric needle or frozen with liquid nitrogen.

20. What year was AIDS first reported in the United States?
    a. 1981
    b. 1977
    c. 1985
    d. 1979

Answers to Sexual Diseases and Disorders

1. c. The Gram stain, a standard laboratory test for gonorrhea, can be administered in a clinic or a doctor's office. For some reason it works better on men than women. The Gram stain gives fairly instant results. Another common test is done by taking a sample of fluid from the infected mucous membrane

(cervix, urethra, rectum, or throat) that is sent to a lab for analysis. Gonorrhea present in either the male or female genital tract can be diagnosed in a lab with a urine specimen.

2. a. When syphilis became widespread at the end of the 15th century in Europe, no one connected it to another virulent disease called yaws, which was later renamed leprosy. Under a microscope, the spirochete causing yaws and causing syphilis appear to be one and the same.

3. b. "The clap" is the street name for gonorrhea, a very common sexually transmitted disease caused by a bacterium called Neisseria. Gonorrhea is spread—usually between younger sexually active people ages 15 to 30—during vaginal or anal intercourse, and oral sex. Gonorrhea can also be passed from mother to child during birth, although this can be avoided by C-section. Described by some men as feeling like "you're pissing razor blades," the clap is characterized by pus-filled discharges from the penis, rectum or vagina. Genitals are feverishly itchy, the rectum burns, and, in females, during menstruation, there is excessive blood. Additionally, the infected person is constipated and it is painful to move the bowels. Luckily, gonorrhea is fairly easily treated by penicillin-derivative antibiotics.

4. a. Impotence is described by the sexual researchers Masters and Johnson in two forms. There is primary impotence, which means the person has never been able to engage in a successful coupling; and secondary impotence, which is described as the failure occurring following at least one successful sexual union. It may be a moot point to the person suffering from this condition, but the treatment approaches vary depending upon whether the impotence is primary or secondary. Hair loss or loads of hair have nothing to do with impotence.

5. b. The Contagious Diseases Act of 1864 in the U.S. was enacted to protect sailors and soldiers in military and naval towns. The act compelled women suspected of carrying a venereal disease to be brought before a magistrate, physically examined, and, if deemed necessary, detained in a designated hospital for treatment. The highly controversial act was repealed in 1886 following the incessant complaining of one Mrs. Josephine Butler, a well-known social reformer.

6. B. Sexual masochism is a bona fide paraphilia, or psychosexual disorder. People who engage in sadomasochistic behavior in their bedroom (or customized torture chamber) are said by psychiatrists to be sexual masochists. For the record, a tribadist is generally a lesbian who has sex by rubbing her clitoris against another person's clitoris; an auto-coprophagist is one who likes to eat their own excrement.

7. d. Kempf's disease is named for Dr. Edward J. Kempf, a psychoanalyst practicing in the 1920s who drew heavily on the theories of Sigmund Freud for his work. The name is a reference to extreme homosexual panic, observed on occasion when a group consisting of only men or women are together for prolonged periods of time. This so-called disorder is thought to be a form of schizophrenia, but it is an unproven theory not embraced by the larger psychological community. The singer/artist Marilyn Manson did a painting and titled it "Kempf's Disease," which popularized the theory again with contemporary audiences. The painting depicts a very pale person with wide, empty eyes who seems either frightened or ashamed.

8. c. Genital herpes is usually caused by Herpes simplex virus type 2. An estimated 30 million Americans are infected. Cold sores, or oral herpes, are most often caused by Herpes simplex

virus type 1. In the United States in the 1980s, the virus spread wildly from coast to coast. An outbreak can include swollen glands, headache, nausea, and pain in the genitals. There may be blisters and open sores on the genitals during an active outbreak. There is no cure for herpes, and once the virus is with you, it is with you forever. Painful outbreaks can be ameliorated by the use of physician-prescribed drugs.

9. d. HPV, or human papillomavirus, is a virus affecting the skin of the genital area in males. In women it attacks the cervix. The virus causes wartlike growths, and skin abnormalities are usually detected during routine internal examinations by one's physician.

10. d. Chlamydia spreads from the vagina into the uterus and up into the fallopian tubes. Symptoms include nausea, cramps during and between menstrual cycles, pain during sex, and pain in the lower back. Males experience a burning sensation upon urination and a whitish drip from the tip of the penis. Chlamydia cannot be spread by kissing, toilet seats, doorknobs, swimming pools, or hot tubs. The only way to get it is during unprotected sex with another person. Three and a half million new cases a year are reported. And a person can have it a long time and not be aware of it.

11. b. Mononucleosis is sometimes called the kissing disease. The disease has nothing to do with kissing. It is an infection caused by the Epstein-Barr virus, and is not transmittable by mouth from one person to another.

12. b. Genital play, masturbation, fantasy, and pleasuring oneself while looking at sexual images all come under the loose psychiatric heading of autoeroticism. Autoeroticism crosses the line into exhibitionism, which, in some cases, is a legal issue.

13. c. Paraphilia is one of the major groups of sexual disorders in the *DSM-IV*. The group ranges widely from minor fetishism, like somebody who's got a thing for blondes or long hair, to the more complex and hard-to-treat problematic disorders like pedophilia, sexual masochism, sexual sadism, voyeurism, and exhibitionism as well as the truly repellent stuff like necrophilia (aroused by dead people), or klismaphilia, which is a sexual fascination with enemas. Paraphiliacs with very mild or minor cases of the condition can even make their ailment work for them. For example, a foot fetishist might happily find his ideal career niche working in a ladies' shoe store.

14. c. Frotteurism is one of the paraphilias. A person who suffers from this disorder has an urge to rub up against people, and derives sexual pleasure from it. Frotteurs adore packed buses, subways, being part of a crush of people, and standing in a crowded elevator.

15. a. Although the word and the idea are today widely denounced by feminists, frigidity remains in the psychiatric literature a true female sexual arousal disorder. It may exhibit itself in deficient or absent sexual fantasy or desire for sexual activity. Aversion to contact with the genitals of another person or a lack of the normal lubrication/swelling response of sexual excitement during sexual activity are the hallmarks of this disorder. While it is currently out of vogue to call a woman frigid, the clinical term exists and there are medical specialists who treat patients for it.

16. c. Coprophilia is one of the many paraphilias. This extremely unappealing condition is characterized by a fascination bordering on obsession with anything involving feces. Coprophiliacs are disgusting, but not that unusual. They have

their own websites, and, bless or curse their little hearts, the Internet has helped bring some of them together.

17. b. Randy Shilts, author of *And the Band Played On*, published in 1987, reported on the AIDS epidemic.

18. c. Rock Hudson, who died on October 2, 1985, of AIDS, or Acquired Immunodeficiency Syndrome, rocked America's definition of who was susceptible to the disease. The truthful reporting of Hudson's condition at the time awakened people to the crisis and made AIDS a household word.

19. True. Anal and genital warts are spread from one partner to another when the affected parts of one partner come in contact with the unaffected parts of the other. The incubation period for this sexually transmitted disease is about six months. A doctor can remove the warts by using an acid, or by electrocautery (electric needle) or cryotherapy (freezing them with liquid nitrogen), but the warts can come back, as the human papillomavirus that causes them can remain in the body indefinitely. Anyone diagnosed with these warts should see a doctor regularly to be checked for them.

20. a. AIDS, or Acquired Immunodeficiency Syndrome, was first reported to the Centers for Disease Control in Atlanta in 1981. By 1984 it had been identified as a human retrovirus, and in 1987 AZT became the first drug approved by the FDA for the treatment of AIDS. Although no longer an automatic death sentence, AIDS continues to be a serious and often fatal disease of the immune system transmitted through blood products, especially through sexual contact or contaminated needles.

Threesomes, Orgies, Gangbangs, and Gender-Benders

Long before the invention of the backyard hot tub or the 1969 screen premiere of the film *Bob & Carol & Ted & Alice*, threesomes, foursomes, and orgies of all descriptions were being enjoyed by randy humans. The great Roman emperors were major orgy-enthusiasts! Today the predilection for being able to sexually experience more than one person at a time grows ever stronger as society's inhibitions about sex continue to subside. Shock-jock Howard Stern has promoted group sex by inviting adult actresses on to his morning radio show to talk about the gangbangs they've participated in. Polyandrous couples (that's four people—two men and two women—who are all "married" to each other) have been interviewed and profiled for national magazines such as *Esquire*. The practical advantages of group sex are obvious: if and when one partner tires out, there's somebody else at the ready who is just getting reignited.

1. What is the French term for a three-way sex scene?
   a. Threesome
   b. Triage
   c. Ménage à trois
   d. Trois ménage

2. What is a Daisy Chain?
   a. An exclusively oral sex act involving three or more partners who simultaneously have their mouths glued to one another's genitals
   b. The participants must be stark naked and the sex acts must take place in a field of grass
   c. All the participants are named Daisy
   d. Flowers are woven in the participants' hair during the sexual congress

3. What is the correct word used to describe a girl–girl sex act where two women try to achieve orgasm by rubbing their clitorises together?
   a. Belly dancing
   b. Bullfighting
   c. Tribadism
   d. Couvade syndrome

4. Where does the word "orgy" come from?
   a. The Greeks, who called it *orgia*, meaning "secret rites"
   b. An Italian word
   c. The Latin for "come together"
   d. An acronym for "orgasm-ready gyrating yoga"

5. How many people need to be participating for group sex to be called a gangbang?
   a. Four
   b. Three
   c. Six
   d. Any number over three

6. Double penetration—or as they call it in the porn movies, a "dp"—means what?
   a. The female has a male member in her vagina and her mouth simultaneously.
   b. The female has a male member in her vagina and her rectum simultaneously.
   c. The female has two male members in her vagina at the same time.
   d. The female has two male members in her mouth at the same time.

7. A man who has had breast implants but has kept his penis can still sexually function as a man under what conditions?
   a. He sees a man who really turns him on.
   b. He has fellatio performed on him for a long time to get him sufficiently aroused.
   c. As long as his nipples are erect, the rest of his sex organs will become erect too.
   d. He is taking a complex series of hormones in order to still be able to have erections even though he is undergoing a sex change.

8. Who was Rene Richards?
   a. The first big transsexual porn star
   b. A transsexual tennis player and surgeon who was not allowed to switch genders in tennis in order to compete as a woman
   c. The doctor who fathered sexual reassignment surgery
   d. The most famous transsexual figure in the 20th century

9. What U.S. city council voted to cover the costs of sex-change operations for its transgender employees, becoming the first city in the nation to do so?
   a. Cleveland
   b. New York City
   c. San Francisco
   d. Miami Beach

10. What is a "key party"?
    a. An on-site gangbang
    b. A party where it is understood that couples will split up for the night and go home with someone else
    c. A keg party with orgiastic sex
    d. A party where the bedroom doors are unlocked and guests are invited to fornicate with each other

11. What was Plato's Retreat?
    a. A legendary swingers' club
    b. A legendary house of prostitution
    c. A legendary Roman orgy playspace
    d. Where Plato himself is said to have had sex

Answers To Threesomes, Orgies, Gangbangs, and Gender-Benders

1. c. The classic French term for a three-way sex scene is *ménage à trois*.

2. a. In a Daisy Chain, three or more partners of any gender arrange themselves so that one person orally services another even as they are being orally serviced. In a perfect Daisy Chain, everyone is mouth to penis, mouth to vagina, and so on and so forth, over and over again. There should be no breaks in the chain. Actual intercourse does not occur in a Daisy Chain; it is limited to oral sex, but not linked to any number of participants. The phrase became part of the American slang vernacular in 1969 during the Summer of Love, when Daisy Chains were noted as something hippies liked to do.

3. c. Tribadism, like frottage, has to do with rubbing genitals together, a masturbatory experience often leading to orgasm. Technically, participants are naked; otherwise it is almost impossible for the two clitorises to meet. Frottage can be experienced fully clothed, although there is no hard-and-fast rule about whether clothes are worn.

4. a. The word "orgy" is believed to come from the Greek word "orgia," meaning "secret rites." The term originally denotes the secret rites or ceremonies connected with the worship of certain deities, especially those of Dionysus-Bacchus. Interestingly enough, the first orgies were restricted only to the fairer sex. Apparently, back in ancient Greece and Rome it was the girls' night to shout!

5. d. Any number of participants over the number three constitutes a gangbang.

6. b. In adult-movie lingo, a "dp," or double penetration, means that a woman has a penis in her vagina and another penis in her rectum at the same time. All that separates the two men is a tiny piece of membrane. Usually they can feel each other's penises moving as they do their own stroke. On a movie set this act requires lube and choreography; it's a hard trick to pull off. At home it is a difficult act, not advised for amateurs. A common position for double penetration is that the woman is on top of one man who has his penis in her vagina; the second man approaches her from behind to penetrate her rectum.

7. d. A pre-op transsexual can still get an erection and use it if he is taking the right combination of hormones. The erection might not be very hard, but men who enjoy the tranny fetish revel in the fact that their partner is able to function as a man and a woman.

8. b. Dr. Rene Richards, who as a man married and fathered a child, was a surgeon who also played on the national tennis circuit. He caused a sensation in the 1970s when he became a she, causing much ink to be spilled on the sports pages about the tennis world's refusal to let him play as a woman. The most famous transsexual figure in the 20th century, however, was Christine Jorgensen, a tireless writer and lecturer on the subject of transsexuality. Jorgensen pleaded for understanding that transsexuals were neither freaks nor perverts.

9. c. In 2003 San Francisco's Board of Supervisors approved a controversial plan to pay for the sex-change operations of trans-

gender city employees, becoming the first city in the nation to do so. The operation can cost $37,000 to transform a man into a woman and $77,000 to turn a woman into a man. But transsexuals need to read the fine print. Only municipal employees are eligible, breast implants aren't covered, and the city won't pay to reduce the size of anyone's Adam's apple.

10. b. A key party, as they were called back in the 1970s, was a party where it was understood that established couples would split up for the night and go home with someone else. The etiquette required men to drop their car keys into a large bowl while the women fished out the keys of the man they wished to go home with. The key party was a short-lived suburban phenomena that hinted there was more to life in suburbia than pickup basketball games and martinis. Ang Lee's 1997 film, *The Ice Storm* starring Christina Ricci, Tobey Maquire, and Sigourney Weaver features a key party scene.

11. a. Plato's Retreat was a New York City Upper West Side swingers' club that existed in the late 1970s and into the early 1980s. It was known to be a fantasyland for frisky fornicators. The fabled club was said to be a regular haunt of Richard Dreyfuss, Sammy Davis, Jr., Jesse Ventura, Rodney Dangerfield, and porn star Ron Jeremy. The famous faces were said to have remained clothed while they ogled the orgy action. Plato's Retreat boasted an enormous swimming pool, a 60-person Jacuzzi, and a cavernous orgy space. The AIDS epidemic cast a pall on it and Mayor Ed Koch cracked down on it, for prostitution. The club closed in 1984. But its legend lives on as various producers take turns pitching it as a movie that has yet to be made.

Strange Sexual Ephemera

MOST PEOPLE don't learn their sexual knowledge from books or classroom study or even from having sex with another individual. Much of what we learn about sex is picked up from snippets of information garnered from TV, radio, tabloid magazines, and the general media. In other words, a lot of our sexual knowledge is just plain trivia. But just because it's trivia doesn't mean it ain't important or true! In this section are questions that test your knowledge of important sexual tidbits. Even if you don't know all the answers, once you memorize them, you'll never be at a loss for fascinating small talk.

1. Which '80s-era NYC downtown personality became famous for her ability to tie her vagina in a knot?
   a. Sharon Mitchell
   b. Kay Parker
   c. Samantha Foxx
   d. Veri Knotty

2. What is the medical name of the condition where a woman has three breasts?
   a. Mondor's disease
   b. Actinomycosis
   c. Polymazia
   d. Mastalgia

3. What male porn star has been celebrated for his ability to suck his own penis?
   a. Joey Silvera
   b. Ron Jeremy
   c. R. Bolla
   d. John Leslie

4. "Bra-buster" Candy Sample's breasts are how big?
   a. 46 inches
   b. 48 inches
   c. 52 inches
   d. 50 inches

5. What European city is considered to be the capital of the modern-day porn business?
   a. Amsterdam
   b. Rome
   c. Vienna
   d. Budapest

6. Which porn star was also a member of the Italian senate?
   a. Rocco Siffredi
   b. Maria Tortuga
   c. Ciccolina
   d. R. Bolla

7. A merkin is:
   a. A secret room in a church used for illicit sex
   b. A helmet used to catch sperm after masturbation
   c. A pubic-hair wig
   d. A cape

8. Which '70s adult movie prominently featured a midget?
   a. *Behind the Green Door*
   b. *The Devil in Miss Jones*
   c. *Deep Throat*
   d. *Mona, the Virgin Nymph*

9. What political symbol was displayed in the movie *Deep Throat*?
   a. The American flag
   b. The swastika
   c. The Liberty bell
   d. The peace sign

10. Who was the first known "squirting girl" in porn?
    a. Fallon
    b. Aunt Peg
    c. Bambi Woods
    d. Nikki Dial

11. Who were Masters and Johnson?
    a. Authors
    b. Inmates
    c. Doctors
    d. S&M performance artists

12. Which '70s male soap opera star performed in adult films and later died after being diagnosed with AIDS?
    a. Harry Reems
    b. Wade Nichols
    c. George Payne
    d. Jack Wrangler

13. What prominent XXX film director once appeared in the 1973 movie *Jesus Christ, Superstar*?
    a. Jamie Gillis
    b. John Holmes
    c. Paul Thomas
    d. Ron Jeremy

14. Andrea True, who appeared in a handful of pornographic films, had a hit single with this song:
    a. "MacArthur Park"
    b. "Ring My Bell"
    c. "Celebrate"
    d. "More, More, More"

15. Before she was a sex therapist, Dr. Ruth Westheimer was:
    a. A psychologist
    b. A sociologist
    c. An educator
    d. All of the above

16. Oscar-winning director Roman Polanski is outlawed from setting foot in America for what reason?
    a. He engaged in bestiality
    b. His connection to Charles Manson
    c. He had sex with a minor
    d. He is a political prisoner

17. Tiny studs set into a pierced penis for the purpose of enhancing sexual pleasure in India are called:
    a. The wooden mortar
    b. Collection of eight balls
    c. The place where four roads meet
    d. All of the above

18. The average amount of semen produced in a solitary ejaculation is:
    a. Two tablespoons
    b. One to two teaspoons
    c. Three-quarters of a teaspoon
    d. One-quarter cup

19. The average number of calories in a teaspoon of semen is:
    a. 7
    b. 6
    c. 3
    d. 25

20. The average number of times a man will ejaculate in his lifetime is:
    a. 4,500
    b. 12,000
    c. 3,700
    d. 7,200

21. The average human sexual experience lasts about how long?
    a. 5 minutes
    b. 11 minutes
    c. 90 minutes
    d. 39 minutes

22. Besides the genitals and the breasts, the only other organ on the human body that routinely swells during intercourse is:
    a. The thymus
    b. The tongue
    c. The soft palate
    d. The inner nose

23. The portion of a man's body women claim to admire the most is:
    a. The butt
    b. The forearms
    c. The hands
    d. The eyes

24. Women who go to college are more apt than high school dropouts to have what kind of sex?
    a. Oral sex
    b. Anal sex
    c. Infrequent sex
    d. A lot of sex

25. Phenylethylamine, the chemical responsible for producing the ecstatic feelings associated with love and sexual attraction, is also found in what foodstuff:
    a. Butter
    b. Chocolate
    c. Strawberries
    d. Mangoes

26. One of the reasons male deer rub their antlers against trees or on the ground is to:
    a. Masturbate
    b. Signal their presence to does in the area
    c. Warn off other males
    d. Sharpen their horns

27. The first known contraceptive was crocodile dung, used by the Egyptians in 2000 B.C. What was it replaced with when they realized it didn't work?
    a. Bee pollen
    b. Beeswax
    c. Deer pellets
    d. Elephant droppings

28. Why did Larry Flynt buy and then decline to publish nude photographs he acquired of Jessica Lynch, she of the Iraqi hospital rescue fame?
    a. He was afraid of lawsuits.
    b. The pictures weren't very appealing.
    c. Lynch wasn't really nude.
    d. He bought them to prevent somebody else from buying them.

29. What exercise regimen/practice is said to improve a person's sex life?
    a. Spinning
    b. Jogging
    c. Yoga
    d. Calisthenics

30. What bizarre, previously unheard-of cosmetic procedure meant to enhance one's sexual attractiveness has swept the West Coast and threatens to become popular in the rest of the U.S.?
    a. Labial piercing
    b. Removing the back molars in order to be able to give better head
    c. Nipple repositioning
    d. Anal bleaching

31. What is the age when it becomes legal for a person to perform in a porn movie?
    a. 21
    b. 18
    c. 19
    d. 16

32. TRUE OR FALSE. Women can ejaculate.

Answers to Strange Sexual Ephemera

1. d. Veri Knotty, porn actress and Greenwich Village personality, was on two counts a rarity in the realm of commercialized sex. First, she was a hawk-nosed brunette in a world of snub-nosed blondes, and second, she had the amazing ability to tie her long, thin labial lips into knots. When Knotty's special talent was revealed, she rocked the socks of porn fans and theatrical performance artists from coast to coast. Knotty enjoyed a long X-rated career, active for seventeen years, sometimes appearing under her other pseudonym, Fanny Wolfe. Her biggest movies were *Centerfold Fever* and *Heatwave*.

2. c. Many women sport an extra nipple, but only 1 out of every 4,000 women has an extra breast. Polymazia or polymastia is a medical condition where a third breast appears somewhere on the body—including in an unusual place, such as in the groin or armpit. The condition is actually more common in men. Ann Boleyn, a wife of Henry VIII, is said to have had it, and yet was considered to be a great beauty. Polymazia is considered to be a congenital abnormality.

3. b. Overweight, hairy, and middle-aged, Ron Jeremy has been a porn-star phenomenon since the 1970s. His often hilarious appearances in over 1,600 adult movies has never deterred him from pursuing his dream as a mainstream actor in legitimate film, where he has appeared playing himself in cameos. A documentary about his unorthodox life called *Pornstar* was released in 2002. Despite his considerable comedic talents, what Jeremy is best known for is his giant penis, so long that he can bend at the middle and orally pleasure himself, even with his protruding, ever-present gut.

4. b. Candy Samples, a legend among big-breast softcore and hardcore porn fans, has been making movies since the 1970s. After being injected with silicone, Candy's boobs measured 48 inches.

5. d. Budapest rules as the European capital of porn. Pornography, long forbidden by the Communists, has become the *de facto* moneymaker in a country that otherwise has been left with few resources. Adult movie companies from all over the world have been fast to move in on the low costs of production and a wealth of low-paid local talent. If porn is an equal opportunity employer, hip to the opportunities of a free market, Budapest has plenty to offer.

6. c. Ciccolina, the toast of Italian porn, once ran as a long shot for the Italian state senate—and won. The voting citizenry was so impressed with Illona Staller's (her real name) irregular credentials that they voted her right in. For a while, Ciccolina was the wife and model of neo-pop artist Jeff Koons, who devoted a sizeable body of work to her. The art exploited kitsch objects, and critics called his work with Ciccolina "an artistic riff on the hyperextension of cuteness towards the pornographic." After the couple split, she returned to working in adult films with another famous Italian actor and director, Rocco Siffredi.

7. c. Counterfeit hair for the private parts, merkins, or pubic-hair wigs, were originally designed for use by those suffering from venereal diseases. Presumably, hair covering the area disguised sores and lesions. Merkins were in popular use during the 1600s; more recently the actress Patricia Arquette wore one in the movie *Human Nature*.

8. a. The Mitchell Brothers' classic *Behind the Green Door*, starring Marilyn Chambers and Johnny Keyes, also had among its kinky and strange cast a midget. The film portrays many people who are far from aesthetically beautiful. But physical beauty, beyond that of Chambers and black superstar stud Johnny Keyes, was beside the point of this Felliniesque sex epic.

9. c. In a sweeping, monumental climax scene in *Deep Throat*, director Gerard Damiano, former hairdresser from Queens turned porn auteur, demonstrated an over-the-top moment of cinematic montage. Among the symbols represented were crashing waves, jungle animals, and the Liberty bell.

10. a. Nobody had ever heard of "squirting" until the appearance of Fallon, a beaky girl-next-door who had one remarkable

talent—the ability to squirt a liquid that was not urine from her vagina. Fallon's female ejaculate inspired endless debate as to whether she was using some kind of device to simulate her unusual secretions. Her reputed ability to produce tangible physical evidence of a female ejaculation drew many fans.

11. a. William Howell Masters was a gynecologist and Virginia Eshelman Johnson was a a psychological researcher. The two teamed up in 1957 to study human sexuality. While Kinsey had asked people to fill out questionnaires about their sexuality, Masters and Johnson did their work as voyeurs and simply watched. Sex—all kinds of sex—was observed in a laboratory setting and then clinically documented. Noted were every raised hair, awakened nipple, and beating heart. The pair measured arousal, tumescence, and orgasm and recorded their findings in their first book, *Human Sexual Response*, published in 1966. The book was at once very popular and very controversial because of the way the authors had gathered their information. The two were married from 1971 to 1993. Johnson retired from the clinic in the early 1990s and Masters died in 2001.

12. b. Wade Nichols, star of *Porn Flakes*, *Barbara Broadcast*, *My Sex-Rated Wife*, and *Summer of Laura*, was also Dennis Parker, an actor and singer with a double life. As a pop singer, he scored a hit with his album "Fly Like an Eagle." As legitimate actor Dennis Parker, he had a recurring role on the soap opera *The Edge of Night*, playing the role of police chief Derrick Mallory from 1979 to 1984. As Wade Nichols, he slipped in and out of the world of porn, making his final film, *Blonde Ambition*, in 1981, after which he was diagnosed with AIDS. Ultimately, Parker (Nichols) chose to take his own life with a gun to avoid the inevitable physical ravages of the disease.

13. c. Paul Thomas is the pseudonym of a well-known porn director responsible for making hundreds of X-rated films. Before he was a porn director, however, he was an adult star who appeared in dozens of XXX films. In an earlier incarnation he was a legitimate actor who appeared in Norman Jewison's movie musical *Jesus Christ Superstar*. Thomas played the role of Peter.

14. d. Andrea True was the leader of her own band, The Andrea True Connection. Her hit song, "More, More, More," asked the all-important question, "How do you like your love?" True, who also went by the *nom de porn* Helen Bed, was an adult actress who was looking for a way to invest $1,400 she'd stashed away in Jamaica. True claims to have written the song in 45 minutes. Unfortunately, "More, More, More" turned out to be her only hit song, although today she is anthologized on shows like VH1's *One-Hit Wonders*, alongside other disco divas like Thelma Houston and Alicia Bridges.

15. d. Dr. Ruth Westheimer is a psychosexual therapist, a psychologist, a sociologist, and a teacher. As a young woman, she left Israel to attend the Sorbonne in Paris, after which she taught kindergarten and studied psychology. In 1956 she immigrated to the U.S. and obtained an M.A. in sociology and a Ph.D. in education from Columbia University. She was mentored by famed sex therapist Dr. Helen Singer-Kaplan at New York Hospital-Cornell University Medical Center. Many became aware of her through her 1980s radio program, *Sexually Speaking*, which made her into a renowned (and often-caricatured) sex therapist.

16 c. It was 1977 when film director Roman Polanski (*Chinatown*, *Rosemary's Baby*) was arrested for the rape of a minor, rape by use of a drug, committing a lewd act on a person under

14 years of age, sodomy, oral copulation, and furnishing drugs to a minor. Polanski had arranged to take photos of the girl, Samantha Geimer, in her swimsuit for French *Vogue* at Jack Nicholson's mansion in Bel Air. After a dip in the hot tub, prosecutors said Polanski gave the girl champagne and Quaaludes and the two had sex. The girl reported the events of the afternoon to her mother, who called the police. Ordered by the court to undergo examination as a "mentally disordered sex offender," Polanski took a plea bargain and acquiesced to one count of unlawful sex with a minor. He faced three years in prison when he fled to France before the sentencing hearing and has not set foot in the United States since. In 2003 he won the Academy Award for his direction of *The Pianist*.

17. d. Tiny studs surgically embedded into the shaft of the penis for the purpose of enhancing sexual pleasure in India are called "the wooden mortar," the "collection of eight balls," and "the place where four roads meet." The idea is that the bumpy texture of the penis will enhance the female partner's sexual pleasure. So far, this is one Eastern-oriented, sexually related practice slow to catch on in the United States.

18. b. One to two teaspoons is the average amount of semen produced in a solitary ejaculation by one man. Ejaculate production varies daily from man to man; some make more, some make less. As long as a man is able to ejaculate, he should consider that a good thing.

19. a. The average number of calories found in a teaspoon of semen is 7. While not exactly as easy on your hips as a zero-calorie cola, swallowing a teaspoon or so of semen once in a while shouldn't affect a diet.

20. d. It has been estimated that the average number of times a man will ejaculate in his lifetime is 7,200.

21. d. The sex researchers and clinicians Masters and Johnson reported that the average human sexual experience lasts 39 minutes.

22. d. The inner nose, fine-tuned to sensation and slight changes and gradations in pulse and body temperature, actually swells a bit during sexual arousal. Check out your lover's face the next time you're making love and watch his or her nose grow . . . in direct proportion to their arousal, that is.

23. a. It's a man's backside that women claim to notice the most when they're checking out male bods.

24. a. According to information gathered for the Kinsey Report, women who attend institutions of higher learning are more likely than high school dropouts to give and receive oral sex.

25. b. Phenylethylamine is the chemical responsible for triggering feelings of ecstasy in the human body most commonly associated with love and sexual attraction. Luckily, it is also a chemical found in chocolate, which is a reason so many people feel chocolate is an aphrodisiac or a substitute for love.

26. a. When a mature buck with a big rack rubs his antlers against trees or against the ground, he's not just trying to scrape off the felt that protects new growth. The animal is also getting an erotic thrill, exciting himself, preparing for the great fornication that lies ahead. The rubbing and scraping of the antlers is a way the

buck stimulates himself before mounting a doe, much in the way a human male might stroke himself before mounting a woman.

27. d. Elephant droppings replaced crocodile dung as an early attempt at contraception in 2000 B.C. The feces—first crocodile, then elephant—were packed high up into a woman's vagina as a kind of repellent mud that was thought to stop sperm from entering the womb. It is hard to believe that anyone would want to have sex under such conditions. The stench, one can only imagine, must have been unbearable.

28. d. On November 11, 2003, Larry Flynt made a statement to the press that he had purchased nude pictures taken in a military barracks of Private Jessica Lynch but that he would never publish them in his magazine, *Hustler*. Saying that "Lynch was used as a pawn by the media and the government to sell the war to America," Flynt went on to say that he "purchased them to keep them out of circulation."

29. c. Yoga, which has been around for about five thousand years, has become a popular exercise activity promoted by health clubs and private yoga teachers all over the Western world. *Time* magazine reported that fifteen million Americans include yoga as part of their fitness regimen. According to Cynthia Worby, M.S.W., author of *The Everything Yoga Book*, practicing yoga improves a person's sex life because circulation is improved, the pelvic floor and organs are toned, the person becomes more flexible, and finally, yoga focuses the mind so that a person can be fully present and in tune with his or her sex partner.

30. d. According to the May 2003 issue of *Vanity Fair* magazine, a hot cosmetic trend sweeping Southern California is the

anal bleach. Los Angeleans are lining up to get their anus bleached to change the natural pigmentation of the skin that most people have between their buttocks. The goal of the bleaching procedure is to lighten the skin so it matches the rest of the person's skin tone. The color brown is frowned upon. Once the trend catches on, no longer will anal sex ever again be referred to as "a brownie."

31. b. You must be 18 years of age and able to prove it to perform in a porn movie—or the film's producers, distributors, and retailers could go to jail over it. Verifying the age of the talent is an ongoing concern in the industry, as underage performers sneak in on a small but indictable scale. In 1986 Traci Lords became news when it was discovered she had used fake I.D. The producers of *Those Young Girls* and Los Angeles porn talent agent Jim South were charged with violating laws prohibiting the use of minors in sexually explicit films. More recently a video called *Sugar Two* was recalled for containing footage of an underage performer, resulting in an FBI and IRS raid on a retailer in Waco, Texas. Federal Code 2257, the Labeling and Record Keeping code, now requires adult companies to ensure that actors and models used in films are not underage.

32. True. Some women can ejaculate! While it is true that some women also urinate slightly at orgasm because the female bladder is located just above the uterus and waves of orgasmic pleasure can cause some loss of control, other women do emit an ejaculatory fluid that is similar in composition to that of a man's except it contains no sperm. It is not yet known what organ in the body manufactures this ejaculate.

Modern
Technological
Breakthroughs

IT'S BREATHTAKING to see how far the technology surrounding sex has come in this century. In just under a hundred years, modern technology has taken us from grinder-house peepshow palaces where one could watch other people having sex on grainy film loops to the wonders of phone sex right up to the Internet. At this very moment, somewhere, sex is being transmitted by satellite. Who knows how far things can go? As you contemplate science fiction and muse on what technological advancement will create the next emerging market, see if you can provide the answers to any or all of these questions.

1. When did organized phone sex get its start?
   a. Around 1970
   b. Around 1980
   c. Around 1990
   d. Ten years ago

2. What famous non-porn-star couple had sex on a tiny movie made specifically for the Internet?
   a. Posh Spice and David Beckham
   b. Pam Anderson and Tommy Lee
   c. Ozzy and Sharon Osbourne
   d. Iman and David Bowie

3. Who is the world's most downloaded Internet woman?
   a. Sunset Thomas
   b. Dani Ashe
   c. Allyssa Milano
   d. Pamela Anderson

4. What piece of technological equipment made real-time reality-show sex with strangers possible right into one's own bedroom?
   a. The VCR
   b. Web cams
   c. Beta/VHS
   d. The digital camera

5. What do you call an on-line community whose primary function is to share information about specific sex and sex acts?
   a. Newsgroups
   b. Chatrooms
   c. Lurker's lounge
   d. Illegal

6. This technology allows computer users to view movies and live sex action on the Internet:
   a. RealPlayer
   b. QuickTime

    c. Windows Media Player

    d. All of the above

7. Virtual reality utilizes which of the following tools for entertaining viewers?

    a. A handheld recorder

    b. A mask

    c. Goggles

    d. Inhaler

8. What technology has displaced VHS tapes as the means of viewing pornography in the home?

    a. Beta tapes

    b. Minicassettes

    c. DVD

    d. Super 8

Answers to Technological Breakthroughs

1. b. In 1983 commercial phone sex was born with the invention of the 900-number line. Callers connected with a number published in a smutty newspaper or magazine, read off a verifiable credit card number, and soon found themselves hooked up to a switchboard, connecting them to either a phone sex operator working in a cubicle in a poorly lit office, or a worker selling aural sex from home. Phone-sex sites began cropping up on the Internet in 1994 when callers were directly connected, rather than having to be rerouted through a dispatcher or a recorded menu. Today 900 numbers are incredibly popular and competition for customers is furious. But it's a cutthroat business. Many phone sex businesses start up—and then sink out of sight without a trace.

2. b. Baywatch babe Pam Anderson and her lover/husband/ex-husband/sometime lover, rocker Tommy Lee, made an XXX film that has been viewed and sold widely over the Internet.

3. b. Internet queen Dani Ashe (she of the 32FF breasts) is the undisputed leader of women downloaded off the Internet. Dani is a celebrity who has been interviewed countless times by Howard Stern. *Hustler Hollywood* sponsored a party to commemorate a replica of her breasts, now available from a company called Topco. Sunset Thomas is the publisher of *Cheri* magazine.

4. b. Web cams, those little cameras you can bring right into your home to broadcast your most intimate moments to your friends and paying customers, revolutionized reality sex and brought a new wave of intimacy to virtual strangers.

5. a. Newsgroups are a way for fans of certain fetishes and sexual functions to come together to discuss their preferences and predilections. Before you join any newsgroup, be aware the FBI may be tracking your movements.

6. d. RealPlayer, QuickTime, and Windows Media Player are three different software packages that basically achieve the same goal. These are tools that enable viewers using different computer operating systems to jointly share in the broadcast and streaming material presented over the Internet. All of this software is available for free download on the company websites, but advanced features cost money.

7. c. Goggles are a tool for providing virtual reality to viewers. Virtual reality is generally considered to be an immersive stereo 3-D display. Virtual Reality was first made famous in mainstream movies and commercials. But for people who are

interested in engaging in the most intense forms of sexual experience, this technology promises to bring sensory pleasures directly to the brain. Not surprisingly, some of the first people to see the possibilities in virtual reality have been pornographers. *Penthouse* magazine was one of the first to try this new terrain. In the vision of this field, which uses the scientific name teledicdonics all types of virtual stimuli will be simulable; cybersex with a virtual or telepresent partner will be the ultimate form of "safe sex," making it the logical evolution from phone sex.

8. c. DVD, or digital video disc, is an optical storage medium with improved capacity and bandwidth compared to the CD or compact disc. DVD, like CD, was initially marketed for entertainment, and later for computer users. DVDs are rapidly becoming the primary way for adult filmmakers and distributors to package their products and deliver them to the marketplace. A DVD can hold a full-length film with up to 133 minutes of high-quality video and audio.

That's Entertainment! Sex in the Culture

ALTHOUGH SOME MAY call the material covered in this section trivial, knowing the way sex has been depicted in the culture is an important part of one's sexual intelligence. From a cultural standpoint, sex is pervasive. You see it on billboards to market blue jeans. Sex helps sell perfume. We are riveted to sexy dialogue and situations on sitcoms and reality TV; we love sexy, button-pushing music videos, sex in literature, sex in cinema, sex on Broadway. An entire museum devoted to sex now exists in New York City. In this part of the quiz, test your knowledge about sex as it has appeared in books, music, film, and the stage. Will these brain-teasing questions identify you as a sexual culture vulture—or someone who's been living under a rock?

1. Who authored the sex manual *Ideal Marriage*?
   a. Max Marcuse
   b. Wilhelm von Humboldt
   c. Van der Velde
   d. Iwan Bloch

2. What controversial Broadway musical featured a number called "Sodomy"?

   a. *Hairspray*
   b. *Hair*
   c. *Boys in the Band*
   d. *Oh! Calcutta!*

3. What sexy novel published in 1969 by Penelope Ashe, supposedly a demure Long Island housewife, is dedicated to "Daddy" and opens with the word "screwed"?

   a. *The Carpetbaggers*
   b. *The Best Laid Plans*
   c. *The Adventurers*
   d. *Naked Came the Stranger*

4. In 1969 Federico Fellini directed *Fellini Satyricon*, depicting the amoral, ancient world of pre-Christian Rome. What 1980 film starring Malcolm McDowell and John Gielgud dealt with similarly perverse material?

   a. *Roma*
   b. *Caligula*
   c. *The Decameron*
   d. *Salo, or the One Hundred Days of Sodom*

5. Who wrote the novel *Memoirs of a Woman of Pleasure*?

   a. John Cleland
   b. David Garrick
   c. The Marquis of Rockingham
   d. Samuel Richardson

6. Which pop tune from the 1960s with incoherent lyrics was rumored to include the "F" word?

   a. "Mrs. Brown, You've Got a Lovely Daughter"
   b. "Jailhouse Rock"
   c. "Satisfaction"
   d. "Louie, Louie"

7. What two middle-aged actors appeared stark naked on stage when the curtain came up in the Broadway show *Frankie and Johnny in the Clair de Lune*?
   a. Antonio Banderas and Mary Stuart Masterson
   b. Edie Falco and Stanley Tucci
   c. Vanessa Redgrave and Brian Dennehy
   d. Kiki and Herb

8. What hard rocker is known for regularly flaunting his naked package on stage?
   a. Anthony Keidis
   b. Iggy Pop
   c. Eminem
   d. Axl Rose

9. In the famous pornographic fable *The Story of O*, what is the chief sexual activity that so shocked readers?
   a. Anal sex
   b. Whipping, flogging, and branding
   c. Oral sex
   d. Blindfolds

10. Who was the Marquis de Sade?
    a. He was a philosopher monk.
    b. He was a sadomasochist.
    c. He was a priest with a vivid imagination.
    d. To date, the real name and life of the Marquis de Sade remains unknown.

11. What was Vladimir Nabokov's great hobby and passion?
    P.S. He was the author of *Lolita*.
    a. Collecting young girls
    b. Collecting reptiles
    c. Collecting butterflies
    d. Collecting human hair

12. Why did R&B legend Marvin Gaye really need "sexual healing"?
    a. He was impotent.
    b. He suffered from premature ejaculation.
    c. He had really bad luck with women.
    d. He was a porn addict.

13. What ghastly sex-related accident happens in *The World According to Garp*?
    a. A woman chokes to death on a penis.
    b. A woman's clitoris is severed in a bizarre cunnilingus incident.
    c. A woman bites off a part of a man's penis while performing oral sex on him in a car.
    d. A man's testicles are crushed by his overenthusiastic lover.

14. Declared "lurid" by the Austin, Texas, school district, this book by Maya Angelou was banned for its depictions of premarital sex and homosexuality. What was the book?
    a. *Singin' and Swingin' and Gettin' Merry Like Christmas*
    b. *I Know Why the Caged Bird Sings*
    c. *The Heart of a Woman*
    d. *Wouldn't Take Nothing for My Journey Now*

15. What former editor of the *Saturday Review* (and author of *A Mad Love* and *Panatopia*, as well as best friend to Oscar Wilde and George Bernard Shaw) is most recalled for his lusty autobiographical memoir, *My Life and Loves*?
    a. Kingsley Amis
    b. Aleister Crowley
    c. H. L. Mencken
    d. Frank Harris

16. What movie directed by Roman Polanski and starring Hugh Grant has a kinky scene featuring a golden shower?
    a. *Basic Instinct*
    b. *Reservoir Dogs*
    c. *Unforgiven*
    d. *Bitter Moon*

17. In the literary magazine *Criterion*, Henry Miller opined that a book written by one of his friends would one day "take its place beside the revelations of St. Augustine, Petronius, Abelard, Rousseau, and Proust." Whose writing was he referring to?
    a. Colette
    b. Anaïs Nin
    c. Pauline Reáge
    d. Sade

18. In what film did Jennifer Tilly and Gina Gershon play a lesbian couple?
    a. *Bound*
    b. *Personal Best*
    c. *Such Good Friends*
    d. *Rocky Horror Picture Show*

19. What actor showed more than his bare behind in Australian director Jane Campion's 1993 movie, *The Piano*?
    a. Richard Gere
    b. Harvey Keitel
    c. Nick Nolte
    d. Al Pacino

20. What was the name of Lady Chatterley's lover?
    a. Sir Clifford Chatterley
    b. Sir Geoffrey
    c. Michaelis
    d. Oliver Mellors

21. In the Japanese import *In the Realm of the Senses*, what sex act shocked censors worldwide into banning the film?
    a. The ingestion of semen
    b. Double-penetration intercourse
    c. Castration
    d. An excrement fetish

22. What rockabilly artist caused a ruckus when he married his thirteen-year-old teenage cousin?
    a. Elvis Presley
    b. Johnny Burnett
    c. Jerry Lee Lewis
    d. Fabian

23. Which musical artist said, "In rock and roll I should be able to do whatever I want—including run around with a dildo on my head"?
    a. Iggy Pop
    b. Eddie Vedder

c. Chris Cornell

d. Flea

24. What tune released by the Starland Vocal Band in 1976 was really an ode to a dish made of spiced shrimp and hot Brie served at a Washington, D.C., cafe, but intimated to listeners they should indulge in daytime sex?

a. "Do That to Me One More Time"

b. "Lady Marmalade"

c. "Afternoon Delight"

d. "Summer in the City"

25. In the novel *Portnoy's Complaint*, what was it that the fictional character Alexander Portnoy repeatedly made love to?

a. The mouth

b. The ear

c. A piece of uncooked liver

d. The mouth of a milk bottle

26. What song written and performed by Marvin Gaye explicitly referred to sex?

a. "Your Precious Love"

b. "Let's Get It On"

c. "Chained"

d. "You're a Wonderful One"

27. Jim Morrison of the Doors was arrested for what crime?

a. Having sex in a public place

b. Having sex with two women in a public place

c. Showing his penis on stage

d. Showing his naked butt on stage

28. What metal rock performer and lead singer for the band Society 1 is also the creator of the porn movie series *Backstage Sluts*?
    a. Nikki Sixx
    b. Matt Zane
    c. Deryck Whibley
    d. Gregg Tribbett

29. What body-pierced, bondage & discipline afficionado musician wrote a kinky autobiography, *The Long Hard Road out of Hell*?
    a. Marilyn Manson
    b. Axl Rose
    c. Tommy Lee
    d. Gene Simmons

30. Who wrote *The Joy of Sex*?
    a. Erich Segal
    b. Harold Evans
    c. Alex Comfort
    d. William Golding

31. What controversial nonfiction book by author Gay Talese described the changing sexual mores of America with its alliterative passages, erotic descriptions, and sweeping historical perspective on sex and censorship?
    a. *Honor Thy Father*
    b. *The Kingdom and the Power*
    c. *Thy Neighbor's Wife*
    d. *The Farbar Case*

32. Legendary writers Bruce Jay Friedman, Mario Puzo, Graham Greene, and Edward "Leggs" McNeil all at one time or

another wrote articles for which notoriously naughty sex and men's adventure magazine?

a. *Gallery*
b. *Genesis*
c. *Stag*
d. *Swank*

33. What iconic female character in literature cried out, "I put my arms around him and drew him down to me so he could feel my breasts all perfume yes and his heart was going like mad and yes I said yes I will Yes"?

a. Mami in Esmeralda Santiago's *Almost a Woman*
b. Miss Kenton in Kazuo Ishiguro's *The Remains of the Day*
c. Molly Bloom in James Joyce's *Ulysses*
d. Xuela in Jamaica Kincaid's *Autobiography of My Mother*

34. In John Updike's novel about suburban-style wife swapping, *Couples*, which adulterous character's underpants wear a "a tender honey stain"?

a. Georgene Thorne, the dentist's wife
b. Foxy Whitman, the wife of the biology professor
c. Angela, the contractor's wife
d. Carol Constantine, the artist

35. Who wrote *Candy*, a 1962 erotically charged spoof of *Candide*?

a. Terry Southern
b. Gore Vidal
c. Charles Bukowski
d. Norman Mailer

36. This novel by a popular author of children's and young adult books who frequently finds her work being challenged in

school districts across the United States was removed from some school libraries for glamorizing sex, and labeled "a sexual how-to." What is the book?

a. *The Princess Diaries* by Meg Cabot
b. *The Face on the Milk Carton* by Carolyn B. Cooney
c. *Forever* by Judy Blume
d. *The Cat Ate My Gymsuit* by Paula Danziger

Answers to That's Entertainment! Sex in the Culture

1. c. Theodore Van der Velde's *Ideal Marriage*, was either written or first published in 1926, although Random House claims to have published it in 1930. *Ideal Marriage: Its Physiology and Technique* is considered to be one of the first modern sex manuals. The book was an instant bestseller although it is hard to find and is almost unheard-of today. For the record, van Humboldt wrote *A History of Whoring*, Marcuse edited a sex journal featuring the writings of Sigmund Freud, including his essay *Hysterical Fantasy and Its Relation to Bisexuality*, and Iwan Bloch was a sexologist who served as advisor for an early film about the problem of syphilis called *Es Werde Licht* (*Let There Be Light*).

2. b. *Hair*, which debuted on Broadway in April of 1968, was a raucous, political show celebrating counterculture. The show was deemed controversial not only for its objection to the Vietnam war, but for its candid commentary on hallucinogenic drugs, celebration of the rock culture, and full nudity as part of the performance.

3. d. On the original book jacket of *Naked Came the Stranger*, a hot novel published in 1969, the author, "Penelope Ashe," is described as a "demure Long Island housewife," photographed

stroking the ears of her Afghan hound. The great hoax was there was no "Penelope Ashe," and the novel was the collaboration of 24 *Newsday* journalists who wrote it as a gag. The book got a terrific second wind when it was translated into a softcore porn movie directed by Radley Metzger and starring Darby Lloyd Rains, released in 1975. The torrid novel, which critics compared to the potboilers of Harold Robbins and Sidney Sheldon, featured dialogue like "Why don't you roll over and see me sometime?" and "I bet you never had a good blow job," prose that urged it on to bestseller lists.

4. b. *Caligula*, the epic-length erotic tale of the rise and fall of decadent ancient Rome, featured eccentric performances and loads of sex and gore. Produced by *Penthouse* publisher Bob Guccione, the film was released in 1981 and ran for several years at an art theater on Manhattan's Upper East Side. It is widely considered to be a movie for lovers of high camp and sexploitation only.

5. a. John Cleland is the author of the most famous erotic novel published in English, *Memoirs of a Woman of Pleasure*, far better known under its more popular title, *Fanny Hill*. Originally published in 1749, it has been banned and shunned by respectable booksellers, seized by authorities, expurgated, and even denounced by its own author, who published it anonymously. *Memoirs of a Woman of Pleasure* failed to receive official recognition for centuries and yet somehow became the most frequently reprinted, translated, and illustrated English novel of all time. The blatantly pornographic tale of a boisterous London prostitute landed a Supreme Court obscenity trial in 1963, instigated by a pioneering edition released in the U.S. that same year. Justice Arthur Klein favorably concluded that while *Fanny Hill* "would never replace *Little Red Riding Hood*, as a popular

bedtime story, it deserved its reputation as an important and honorable work."

6. d. The Kingsmen had a hit with "Louie, Louie," a song featuring lyrics very few people could understand. The song became a cult phenomenon at parties, where people hovered around the record player, straining their ears. Did they hear what they thought they were hearing? The Smoking Gun website reported that complaints from the parents of teenagers and others sent the FBI scurrying to determine if the lyrics violated federal obscenity laws. The G-men slowed the 45-rpm single down to 33⅓ but never could prove that the "F" word was actually said.

7. b. In Terrance McNally's production of *Frankie and Johnny in the Clair de Lune*, Edie Falco and Stanley Tucci shocked audiences when they appeared stark naked when the curtain first comes up. After the show played for a few months, it was revealed that Tucci and Falco were "an item." Rosie Perez and Joe Pantoliono took over when Falco and Tucci retired from the roles.

8. b. Aging legend Iggy Pop is best known for being the grandfather of punk, but equally known for showing everything he's got (although not in full tumescence) on stage. He has been arrested many times.

9. b. In the pornographic novel *The Story of O*, sadomasochism is what both excited and upset readers. Every sort of sadomasochistic activity, including blindfolds, piercings, whippings, floggings, and brandings, is inflicted on O. *Newsweek* heralded the book as "a mystic document." Readers were shocked yet mesmerized by the primary theme of abuse and its transcendent effect on the female protagonist.

10. d. The true identity and much of the life of the Marquis de Sade remains a riddle. Born into a noble house, at the age of 23 he was forced into an arranged marriage to a wealthy woman. He was discovered by his mother-in-law and sister-in-law carousing with prostitutes and imprisoned without a trial, where he remained for fourteen years. During the Terror, his life was spared and he became a revolutionary who only narrowly escaped the guillotine only to be later arrested. His friends and his enemies alike strived to burn most of his writings, trying to erase his name from history. The last twelve years of his life were spent in an insane asylum at Charenton, where he mounted plays starring both professional actors and the inmates. The author of *Justine* and *Philosophy in the Bedroom* died at Charenton in the arms of his teenage mistress. Although he is often called Donatien Alphonse Francois de Sade, his real name remains unknown.

11. c. Born into an aristocratic Russian family, Vladimir Nabokov grew up on a great estate. As a child, he collected butterflies, collecting over seventy species. His first published work was a scientific paper in a journal called *The Entomologist*. Arriving in the U.S. in 1940 after the Nazis invaded France, Nabokov secured work classifying and drawing butterflies for the Museum of Natural History. He was a visiting professor of etomological studies at Harvard and later became a professor of Russian and European literature at Cornell, remaining there for ten years. During the summers, he continued to collect butterflies and wrote *Lolita*. Experiencing difficulty finding a publisher, in 1955 he took the book to France, which didn't help. Rejected by American publishers, banned by the government of France, pronounced as "objectionable," by the U.S. Customs office, *Lolita* became a bestseller three years later in 1958 when it was published by G.P. Putnam, enabling Nabokov to abandon

teaching to write full time. The story of a middle-aged pervert and his obsession with a twelve-year-old girl, *Lolita* is at heart a parody and a satire of the romantic novel. Two movies were made from Nabokov's novel, the first directed by Stanley Kubrick in 1962 starring the then-fourteen-year-old Sue Lyon, the second in 1998 starred Dominque Swain and was directed by Adrian Lyne.

12. d. Marvin Gaye was a porn-aholic who couldn't resist collecting S&M films, had a large personal collection of pornography, and was addicted to the works of French bondage cartoonist Georges Pichard. Finding this so startling, David Ritz, Gaye's biographer, said while visting the musician at his home in Belgium, "You need sexual healing." Gaye never got healed. Instead, he was shot to death at home by his father.

13. c. Amputations, maimings, and scenes that practically throb with phallic resonance are the literary hallmarks of John Irving, who also authored *A Prayer for Owen Meany, Cider House Rules, A Widow for a Year, The Fourth Hand*, and *The Hotel New Hampshire*. In an inspired scene in *The World According to Garp*, three-fourths of Garp's penis is neatly chomped off during an accident that has Garp's two children in the car while Garp's lover, Helen, is administering a blow job. As a result of the accident, Helen bites off most of her own tongue, one of Garp's sons is killed, and the other is blinded. Garp's own jaw is broken.

14. b. Although Maya Angelou has been hailed as one of the great voices of contemporary literature, the internationally respected poet, writer, and educator has been attacked and assailed and even banned by librarians, teachers, and entire school districts for her candid descriptions of sex. *I Know Why the Caged Bird Sings* is the first of five volumes of Angelou's

autobiography, dealing with early aspects of her life up to age sixteen. The narrator and main character endures a harrowing rape and expresses and acts out her self-loathing. The true themes of the book are abandonment and racial segregation, but the book contains explicit sections about premarital sex and homosexuality as well.

15. d. It wasn't just the written work of former editor of the *Saturday Review* Frank Harris (1855–1914) that was scandalous. Widely regarded as a mythic carouser, Harris married no less than three times and was a notorious liar and braggart. Reviewers sometimes asked of Harris's work, "Is this a novel or a confession?" An unlikely sexual conqueror, the man was puny, ugly, and possessed a famously low forehead. The first volume of *My Life and Loves* was published in Berlin; eventually there would be five volumes. Years earlier Harris had attempted to sell the first portion of his autobiography in France, only to have the manuscript seized by the authorities. His main partner in sexual crime (only a slight exaggeration), was his friend Aleister Crowley, whose name is synonymous with ceremonial magick.

16. d. The controversial "golden showers" scene in exiled director Roman Polanski's 1992 feature *Bitter Moon*, starring Peter Coyote, Hugh Grant, and Kristin Scott-Thomas (the two were also together in *Four Weddings and a Funeral*), is explicit. But even softcore pornography and sexual freakiness weren't enough of a draw to make this film a hit. Marketed as an art film, *Bitter Moon* lives on in the annals of fetish-film afficionados. Hugh Grant, by the way, never gets naked.

17. b. For more than three decades Anaïs Nin kept a detailed and highly personal journal that became the object of much speculation and gossip. Nin occasionally regaled close friends in

Paris with tidbits from her diary. Among them was her pal and fellow writer, Henry Miller. In the English magazine *Criterion*, Miller wrote that Nin's journals would become famous. The prodigious diarist managed to produce some 150 volumes of transcript, more than 15,000 pages. Eventually seven volumes of her diary were published in addition to her other works, including *The Four-Chambered Heart*, *A Spy in the House of Love*, and *Henry and June*.

18. a. Any movie that opens with a scene of a woman tied up and locked in another woman's closet is bound to be an eyebrow-raiser. *Bound*, released in 1996, is a male sexual fantasy about two women in a lesbian relationship. The camera slowly circles the bed that Gershon and Tilly lie in with close-ups of Gershon's various body parts steamy enough to make men and lesbians weep. It's a bloody movie, too, which is also interesting since *Bound* also stars Joe Pantoliano of *Sopranos* fame. Joey loses blood in this show, too.

19. b. Not a bit shy about acting in the nude, Harvey Keitel revealed full frontal nudity in Jane Campion's tale about a mute pianist and her brash lover. *The Pianist* was not Keitel's first totally nude scene. He also showed his penis in *The Bad Lieutenant*, a 1991 film directed by Abel Ferrara.

20. d. Oliver Mellors, the estate's gamekeeper, was Lady Chatterley's lover. *Lady Chatterley's Lover* was D. H. Lawrence's final novel. Privately published in Florence in 1928, the book underwent the censor's knife to be republished in England in 1932. Grove Press undertook the printing of an unexpurgated version in America in 1959. The bittersweet story of an unhappy marriage and physical love affair and a child borne out of wedlock, *Lady Chatterley's Lover* follows the life of Constance

(Connie) Reid, who marries Sir Clifford Chatterley. Shortly after their marriage, Chatterley is wounded in the war and confined to a wheelchair. He no longer can have sex. Sexually stifled by her husband's injuries, Connie first has a brief, unsatisfactory affair with her husband's friend, the playwright Michaelis, but soon finds herself in a passionate physical relationship with Oliver Mellors, the estate's gamekeeper. Falling pregnant, she travels to Italy to disguise the true parentage of her child. The book was vilified for its glorification of sexual relationships, and for its explicit language and content.

21. c. Released in 1976, Nagisa Oshima's sexual opus, *In the Realm of the Senses*, remains one of the most controversial films in the world. Banned in many nations, it's too explicit even for cable. A portrait of sexual obsession, *In the Realm of the Senses*, is the story of a man and a prostitute, whose liaison grows more dangerous with every encounter. In the final, terrifying scene, the woman castrates her lover. Like Oshima's 1968 film, *Death by Hanging*, the story of *In the Realm of the Senses*, was inspired by true headlines of love run amok that ran in the more lurid Japanese newspapers. In Japan there is a cult and a fetishism of the phallus, as it represents and embodies the hopes and desires for potency and fertility. Large stone phalluses are commonplace and are clung to and kissed by women. What people in America and Europe found shocking about *In the Realm of the Senses* is much better understood and appreciated in Japan.

22. c. Jerry Lee Lewis was a self-proclaimed rompin', stompin' piano-playing son-of-a-bitch singer who took as his second wife his thirteen-year-old cousin, Myra Gale Brown. Lewis had already been married for a year and a half to his preacher's daughter, and the divorce wasn't final when he married Myra Gale. A month after the wedding Myra Gale gave birth to Jerry

Lee's son, Jerry Lee, Jr. In the movie version of Jerry Lee's life, *Great Balls of Fire*, Dennis Quaid starred as Jerry Lee and Winona Ryder played the teenage bride.

23. b. It was Eddie Vedder who told *Rolling Stone* magazine that in rock and roll he should be able to do whatever he wants to do, including run around with a dildo on his head.

24. c. Bill and Kathy Danoff, who wrote and performed the song "Afternoon Delight," were a clean-cut all-American couple on the folkie circuit. The song is really dedicated to a culinary repast the couple enjoyed eating at Clyde's in Washington, D.C. But it did hint at sex.

25. c. Probably one of the funniest, although not the most terribly erotic, scenes in the angst-ridden sexcapade novel *Portnoy's Complaint* is the sexually frustrated teenage boy Alexander Portnoy's encounter with his family's uncooked supper. Having abandoned his habit of masturbating into his sister's soiled underpants, conveniently discovered in the bathroom hamper, the acne-prone, hormonally charged teenager desperately deposits his seed into a slice of uncooked calves' liver. Mercifully, he remembers to wash it off in the kitchen sink before returning it to the meat drawer, thinking as he twirls a piece of it on the end of his fork hours later that only a few hours before, he'd had it neatly wrapped around his penis.

26. b. The suggestive lyrics and crooning, soulful voice of Marvin Gaye's epic number-one hit, "Let's Get It On," was a direct homage to sex.

27. a. At a Doors concert in New Haven, police arrested Morrison for having sex before the show in a shower. Morrison

resisted arrest as his manager Bill Siddons pleaded with the police to let him do the show. Later the legendary sexual figure and rocker was taken to Court Street and booked for breaching the peace, resisting arrest, and for immoral exhibition. He was released on $1,500 bail. Charges were eventually dropped and Morrison paid a $25 fine.

28. b. Hard rocker Matt Zane, best known for his dramatic stage act of inserting meat hooks through the skin of his back and then suspending himself in the air, is also the creator of *Backstage Sluts*, a porn series that showcases hard rock bands and bad babes getting down and dirty on tour buses.

29. a. Marilyn Manson is the author of *The Long Hard Road out of Hell*. He is a multi-pierced bondage and discipline quasi-expert as well as an established artist and musician.

30. c. Alex Comfort was the author of *The Joy of Sex*. Published in 1972, Comfort's paean to the delights of the bedroom became one of the best-selling sex books of all time. A 30-year-anniversary edition was published in 2003.

31. c. *Thy Neighbor's Wife*, published in 1980, was author Gay Talese's breakthrough book on sexuality. The book was a terrific financial success even as critics bashed it for failing to include all aspects of sexuality, including homosexuality, incest, venereal disease, and contraception, as well as for Talese's overt suggestion that women are second-class citizens. Reviewers noted that, for a sex book, the prose was rather dry and joyless. Nonetheless, *Thy Neighbor's Wife* opens with a scene of masturbation and recounts much marital infidelity and names actual names (where permission had been given) of the participants.

32. d. The humorist writer Bruce Jay Friedman, respected novelists Mario Puzo and Graham Greene, and noted punk-rock culture writer and author of *Please Kill Me*, Edward "Leggs" McNeil all at one point or another in their careers were contributing writers to *Swank* magazine. Bruce Jay Friedman, in fact, was the editor in chief of the publication for a brief stint in the late 1960s.

33. c. It is Molly Bloom, the horny opera-singing wife of Leopold Bloom, advertising agent, who closes Joyce's famous novel with her long, exuberant soliloquy that ends in a joyous, carnal libretto. Widely regarded to be a life-affirming endnote to an often dreary and difficult book, the scene has also been described as orgasmic. What could be more life-affirming than fantasizing and getting oneself off?

34. a. It is Georgene Thorne, the dentist's wife and lover of Piet Hanema, whose underpants wear "a tender honey stain." That stain is from drips of urine, not feminine secretions caused by sexual arousal. For some reason Georgene's soiled underwear is a turn-on to her lover, not a turn-off.

35. a. Novelist and screenwriter Terry Southern once said his mission in life was to "attack smugness." In his role as a satirist and king of hip sex and dark humor, Southern reveled in his role as the quintessential artist of the counterculture. Wearing dark sunglasses, Southern appears behind John Lennon on the cover of *Sgt. Pepper's Lonely Hearts Club Band*. For kicks, he hung out with Peter Fonda and Dennis Hopper. Decades before reality TV, he invented a game show called *What's My Disease? Candy* is the epitome of cool porn. Its heroine, Candy Christian, wants to lose her virginity to her father's Mexican gardener, but

instead falls into the mysterious sexual netherworld of her college professor, Dr. Mephesto, and a peculiar Dr. Krankeit. The book is a carnal carnival, hilarious and a fast read.

36. c. *Forever* by Judy Blume is a tale of first love. Katherine, the girl, loves Michael, the boy, so much that she decides to give her virginity to him. Blume rocked some boats by her depiction of a character who is a sexually active teen. Intimate details about first-time sex are spelled out, a factor that landed Blume on the banned list at the library at Frost Junior High in Schaumburg, Illinois, and other school districts as well.

Sex and the Law

Engaging in or dealing in sex can sometimes send a person to the Big House! One minute you're rockin' and rollin' and the next minute someone is putting the cuffs on you. To steer clear of the law, knowing it can help you avoid a whole heap of trouble. When it comes to fornicating or dealing in fornication, just remember one basic rule which any judge will be glad to repeat for you. "Ignorance is no excuse."

The following two segments of the quiz deal with issues of sexual legality. The first segment, "It's On the Books," raises questions on existing laws in a variety of places you may or may not ever visit where a person can easily run afoul of the law. "Famous Obscenity Cases" tests your knowledge of U.S. Supreme Court decisions involving obscenity. Hopefully you will never need to experience firsthand the ramifications of these laws—but if you happen to be a lawyer or a legal crackpot, your expertise undoubtedly will give you a leg up on enhancing your overall score!

It's On the Books

Strange rules in strange places—how many of these laws do you know that'll keep you clear of trouble?

1. In accordance with the rules of Islam, no Muslim may look at the private parts of dead people. This law also applies to:
   a. Doctors
   b. Undertakers
   c. Nurses and other medical personnel
   d. All of the above

2. A male doctor in the Middle Eastern country Bahrain may examine the genitals of a female patient under what provision?
   a. He may conduct his examination only by studying the genitals as they appear reflected in a mirror.
   b. He is allowed to examine the genitals of a female patient if a woman with a medical degree or background is in the room.
   c. He may examine the genitals of a female patient only if she is moments away from giving birth.
   d. He may examine the genitals of a female patient if she is an infant who has just been born.

3. Where is it legal in the state of Maryland for condoms to be sold from vending machines?
   a. Condoms may be sold in vending machines that do not offer other items including cigarettes.
   b. Condoms may be sold in vending machines that are 100 yards from school or government premises.
   c. Condoms may be sold in places where alcoholic beverages are sold for consumption on the premises.
   d. Condoms may not be sold in vending machines in the state of Maryland at all

4. Men are permitted to have sexual intercourse with animals in Lebanon if the animal partner is female. If the animal partner happens to be male, and the pair are caught, what is the punishment meted out to the human?

   a. There is no punishment to the human but the animal may be executed and eaten.

   b. The male animal's natural partner gets to bite, kick, or claw the offending human who took advantage of her partner.

   c. The human must pay money to the male animal's owner.

   d. Death is the punishment meted out to the unlucky human caught having sex with a male animal.

5. What local city council in what California community recently repealed its anti-adultery statutes, punishable by a sentence of up to three months in jail?

   a. Beverly Hills

   b. Rolling Hills

   c. Agoura Hills

   d. San Marino

6. TRUE OR FALSE. It is illegal to have sex with a corpse anywhere in the United States.

7. In the United States, what are the so-called "crimes against nature"?

   a. Oral or anal sex with another person

   b. Having sex with an animal

   c. Masturbation

   d. Incest

8. What is meant by the term "blue law"?
   a. They are laws on the books that specifically prohibit sexual activities on Sundays.
   b. They are laws which prohibit prostitution or lewd or topless dancing establishments to exist.
   c. They are state and local regulations which ban certain activities on the day of the Sabbath.
   d. They are establishments catering to sexual entertainment and that are required by law to be regulated by "men in blue," i.e. the police.

9. What social satirist and comedian was arrested time and again on obscenity charges?
   a. Godfrey Cambridge
   b. George Carlin
   c. Lenny Bruce
   d. Richard Pryor

Answers to It's On the Books

1. d. In the Muslim religion, no one, not even a doctor or an undertaker, is allowed to let their gaze wander over the private parts of a dead person. If you are a male doctor, you also may not be caught directly looking at the private parts of a living woman (unless she is your wife)!

2. a. There is no reason or circumstance for a male doctor in Bahrain, a country in the Middle East, to directly examine the genitals of a female patient. The only way he can examine them is to study their reflection in a mirror.

3. c. A condom can be bought from a vending machine in Maryland as long as alcoholic beverages, meant to be consumed on the spot, are sold on the premises as well.

4. d. Death is the absolute punishment for any human caught fornicating with a male animal in Lebanon. A human caught fornicating with a female animal is either ignored or applauded.

5. b. In April of 2003 the incorporated community of Rolling Hills, California, finally repealed its adultery statutes, largely in an effort to trim the city budget. All the members of the town council, it should be noted, were married at the time the statutes were rescinded.

6. True. It is never legal for anyone for any reason to have sex with a corpse in the United States.

7. a. The so-called Crimes Against Nature belong to Section 14-177 of the North Carolina General Statutes, which are derived from an English statute passed during the reign of Henry VIII. "CAN" as it is called, is "sexual intercourse contrary to the order of nature" and "all acts of bestial character whereby degraded and perverted sexual desires are sought to be gratified." In essence this means fellatio and cunnilingus (oral sex) and anal intercourse. The law has been held up time and time again by judges in North Carolina, although the June 26, 2003 ruling by the Supreme Court issuing a sweeping declaration of constitutional liberty for gay men and lesbians overrules all current sodomy laws, making certain so-called "crimes against nature" perfectly acceptable.

8. c. Blue laws are state and local regulations that ban certain activities such as sales, work, or sport on Sundays. The term is believed to have derived from the blue paper on which some 17th-century laws were printed. Although they are not often enforced, many states retain these laws.

9. c. Lenny Bruce (1926–1966) was an American comedian whose obscene and scathing humor got him repeatedly charged with obscenity. He was arrested at the Jazz Workshop in San Francisco in 1961 for violating the California Obscenity Code. The word "cocksucker" was part of his routine. In 1962 he was arrested at the Troubador Theatre in Hollywood, California, for saying the word "motherfucker." In 1964 he was arrested for obscenity at the Café Au Go Go in New York City. His trials are considered now to be landmark cases in the fight to preserve freedoms set forth in the First Amendment. The poets Allen Ginsberg, Gregory Corso, Laurence Ferlinghetti, writers James Baldwin, Joseph Heller, Henry Miller, Gore Vidal, and singer Bob Dylan drew up and signed a petition protesting the use of the New York obscenity laws to harass a controversial social satirist. Bruce's last performance was in 1966 at the Fillmore Auditorium in San Francisco where he played on the same bill as Frank Zappa and The Mothers of Invention. He is famous for saying (among other things) "Take away the right to say 'fuck' and you take away the right to say 'fuck the government.'"

Famous Obscenity Cases

From time to time the subject of obscenity—usually in the form of a book or a movie or performance art—wends its way to the Supreme Court. With all the real trouble in the world, it's hard to believe anybody really cares about sex so much. And yet the issue of obscenity is a serious one—just ask any robed justice!

1. Which classic modern novel formed the basis of obscenity decisions in the United States?
   a. *This Side of Paradise* by F. Scott Fitzgerald
   b. *The Jungle* by Upton Sinclair
   c. *From Here to Eternity* by James Jones
   d. *Ulysses* by James Joyce

2. The following is the standard for determining if material is obscene:
   a. The average person finds the work appeals to prurient interest
   b. The work describes prohibited sexual conduct defined by individual state law
   c. The work lacks serious literary, artistic, political, or scientific value according to community standards
   d. All of the above

3. Which amendments to the U.S. Constitution have been used to defend obscenity cases?
   a. The First and the Sixth
   b. The First and the Twelfth
   c. The First and the Fourteenth
   d. The Second

4. How did a *Hustler* magazine cartoon depict evangelist Jerry Falwell in the case that went before the Supreme Court?
   a. Giving Larry Flynt oral sex
   b. As praying to Mohammed
   c. Receiving a gift of a dildo from the Devil
   d. Having drunken sex with his mother in an outhouse

5. Which Supreme Court justice relied on the First Amendment to rule on cases of obscenity?
   a. William Rehnquist
   b. William O. Douglas
   c. John Jay
   d. Clarence Thomas

6. What reformer during the 19th century in America greatly influenced the direction of legal obscenity cases?
   a. Horace Greeley
   b. Anthony Comstock
   c. Jane Adams
   d. W. E. B. Du Bois

7. What did a New York judge say about *Deep Throat* before fining an adult movie house in New York City 3 million dollars?
   a. "Jesus would find this obscene."
   b. "The movie is a feast of carrion and squalor."
   c. "I enjoyed the film but it's clearly obscene."
   d. All of the above

8. What was Larry Flynt's punishment as a result of the *Hustler Magazine v. Falwell* decision?
   a. He had to pay Falwell $500,000.
   b. He was let off the hook.
   c. He went to jail for six months.
   d. He was shot.

9. What famous photographer's works were the basis for a 1990 obscenity charge involving the Contemporary Arts Center in Cincinnati, Ohio?
   a. Thomas Condon
   b. Helmut Newton
   c. Robert Mapplethorpe
   d. Veronique Vial

Answers to Famous Obscenity Cases

1. d. James Joyce's *Ulysses* had a troubled legal history. On December 6, 1933, a U.S. District Court in New York granted a decree dismissing a suit against *Ulysses*. It was judged that the reputation of the book in the literary world was so great that any pornographic elements in it were secondary to the novel's literary merits.

2. d. In the United States, the Constitutional standard for determining whether or not a material—be it a book, film, play, or live performance—is obscene is if the average person finds the work appeals to a prurient interest. A work may be called obscene if the material describes some sexual conduct prohibited by state law, and if the work is deemed to be utterly lacking in literary, artistic, political, or scientific value. All of this, obviously, leaves a great deal of room for argument and interpretation.

3. c. The right to free speech of the First Amendment and the due process clause of the Fourteenth Amendment are most often invoked to defend obscenity cases. The key Supreme Court decision regarding obscenity is considered to be a case known as *Miller v. California*, which was decided in 1973 after Miller, a seller of dirty books, was arrested. His defense took years to work its way through to the Supreme Court. The defendant was ultimately exonerated.

4. d. A famous *Hustler* magazine cartoon depicted evangelist Jerry Falwell fornicating with his mother—in an outhouse. The case made it all the way to the Supreme Court, which ruled that *Hustler* had every right to mock Jerry Falwell because the mocking was clearly done in a satirical fashion.

5. b. William O. Douglas is considered to be the best friend of the First Amendment for his outspoken persistence in promoting free speech. He is famous for this quotation: "Restriction of free thought and free speech is the most dangerous of all subversions. It is the one un-American act that could most easily defeat us."

6. b. During the 1870s in America, Anthony Comstock was the reformer best known for influencing obscenity cases in the courts. Convinced that his critics were "under Satan's power," he prayed earnestly to save those wicked men and women who indulged in obscenity and drank and swore. Comstock banned any depiction, no matter how indirect, of the act of intercourse. Comstock's influence reigned in New York City as he incorporated, with his backers, the New York Society for the Suppression of Vice. The term "Comstockery" was synonymous with "prudery."

7. b. According to porn journalist Luke Ford, regarding *Deep Throat*, in 1972 Judge Joel E. Tyler of New York said, "The movie is a feast of carrion and squalor," and ruled it obscene. His punishment? To fine the World Theatre where it was playing a cool $3 million. Ford reported that after Tyler retired from the bench, he wrote, "If I were to make that decision today, I would be deemed a fool."

8. b. Larry Flynt was shot by an antiporn fanatic, an incident which has consigned him to life in a wheelchair. However, as a result of the lawsuit, *Hustler Magazine v. Falwell*, Flynt was let off the hook and allowed to keep on publishing obscene cartoons.

9. c. A case regarding a retrospective of Robert Mapplethorpe's controversial nudes at the Contemporary Arts Center in Cincinnati in 1990 went all the way to the Ohio Supreme Court. Charges of obscenity were dropped because the photographs were judged to be works of art. In 2003 Thomas Condon ran afoul of the same set of Ohio laws for his artistic representations of dead bodies, which has been called "corpse abuse." The subjects of Condon's photographs aren't naked, they're just dead, but that is considered an obscenity.

Sexual Personalities

IF YOU ARE very knowledgeable about sex culture and a devoted reader of tabloids, you'll do very well on this portion of the quiz and have a chance to show off your wonderfully particular knowledge! Some of the most easily recognized names in the world appear in this segment, as well as some important individuals whose personal stories and contributions to sex have been shelved and forgotten. Here's a chance for you to toast those folks again—and gain more points for your final score while you're lauding them.

1. Which gay actor starred in the revolutionary adult movie *Boys in the Sand*?
   a. Casey Donovan
   b. Harry Reems
   c. John Holmes
   d. Rick Hollander

2. Who was the "Happy Hooker"?
   a. Sidney Biddle Barrow
   b. Xaviera Hollander
   c. Heidi Fleiss
   d. Roxanne Pulitzer

3. Who was Polly Adler?
   a. She was an anthropologist who studied the sexual habits of aboriginal people.
   b. She was television's first sex talk host.
   c. She was a brothel owner summoned by the New York City D.A.'s office in the 1930s in an effort to bust the Mob.
   d. She invented the first sex toy.

4. What was the psychiatrist Wilhelm Reich's great contribution to sexual science?
   a. He advocated vasectomy as a method of birth control.
   b. He identified the gene predisposing a person to homosexuality.
   c. He revitalized and modified ancient Eastern sexual practices for use in mid-19th-century Germany.
   d. He invented the Orgone Box, a device claimed useful for measuring orgasms.

5. This coproducer of the famous X-rated movie *Debbie Does Dallas*, was also a cofounder of *Screw* magazine. Who is it?
   a. Jann Wenner
   b. Jim Buckley
   c. Bob Guccione
   d. Bill Ayers

6. The 1930s actress and comedienne Mae West was in a play that was banned for its sexual content. What was the play called?
   a. *Come Up and See Me Sometime*
   b. *What's That in Your Pocket?*
   c. *Myra Breckinridge*
   d. *Sex*

7. Which popular vaudeville star was a renowned cross-dresser who later had a theater in Times Square named after him?
   a. Bert Williams
   b. Julian Eltinge
   c. Eddie Cantor
   d. Milton Berle

8. Which famous American author scandalized the public by taking up and sporting with a 13-year-old girl?
   a. Nathaniel Hawthorne
   b. Edgar Allen Poe
   c. Upton Sinclair
   d. Stephen Crane

9. Which big box-office male movie star's career was ruined when a minor actress died after fleeing his hotel room? Reportedly she had a glass bottle stuck in her vagina.
   a. Ramon Navarro
   b. Rudolph Valentino
   c. Fatty Arbuckle
   d. Charlie Chaplin

10. This Roman emperor got his kicks from swimming in a pool with little boys and girls in Capri. Who was it?
    a. Tiberius
    b. Julius Caesar
    c. Marcus Aurelius
    d. Hadrian

11. This former German convent girl who wanted to be an actress became mistress to Adolph Hitler. Who was she?
    a. Sonja Henie
    b. Lina Wertmuller
    c. Eva Braun
    d. Lotte Lenya

12. In the early 1940s what handsome Canadian airman murdered his beautiful New York City society wife in a scandalous gay love triangle?
    a. Jack Mortimer
    b. Robert Wagner
    c. Hank Bauer
    d. Wayne Lonergan

13. A sensualist in the extreme, Russian Empress Catherine the Great was said to enjoy congress in this fashion.
    a. She craved sex with horses.
    b. She wanted to get it on with dogs.
    c. Anal sex was Cathy's thing.
    d. Asphyxiafilia.

14. In his day, this black-eyed Russian court figure was the love object of all Russian society, both cultured and crude. Who was this mesmerizer?
    a. Leo Tolstoy
    b. Trotsky
    c. Aleksandr Kerensky
    d. Rasputin

15. What '60s-era sitcom star went down the tubes as a result of his sordid sexual lifestyle?
    a. Dick York
    b. Bob Crane
    c. Carl Betz
    d. Jerry Paris

16. Pee Wee Herman was arrested for what crime?
    a. He was caught having sex with a minor.
    b. He was arrested in a gay porn Internet sting.
    c. He got caught shoplifting from a sex toy shop.
    d. He got caught masturbating in a movie theater.

17. This sleazy Cleveland businessman is generally considered to be the "father" of the peep show. Who was he?
    a. Sam Giancana
    b. Lou Peraino
    c. Dennis Kucinich
    d. Reuben Sturman

18. What very married presidential front-runner resigned from a hot race when it was revealed he had been having an extramarital affair?
    a. Gary Hart
    b. John Anderson
    c. Mike Dukakis
    d. Ross Perot

19. What household product was Marilyn Chambers promoting during her early tenure as a porn star?
    a. She was selling toilet paper.
    b. She was pushing tissues.
    c. Paper towels were being hawked.
    d. Marilyn was box-cover girl for some laundry detergent.

20. What TV producer long associated with *The Sixty-Four-Thousand-Dollar Question* evaded jail time and went on to become the publisher of *Penthouse Forum* magazine?
    a. Harry Friedman
    b. Albert Z. Freedman
    b. Bert Convey
    d. Merv Griffin

21. What naughty publication ran indiscreet photographs of Miss America Vanessa Williams, resulting in the loss of her crown?
    a. *Celebrity Skin*
    b. *Penthouse*
    c. *Hello!*
    d. *Cheri*

22. John Curtis Holmes, a.k.a. Johnny Wadd, lost his virginity at the age of 12 to a 36-year-old pal of his mother. By his own reckoning, John possessed a ten-inch penis. How many women did he claim to service with it—both on- and off-screen—in his lifetime?
    a. 500
    b. 1,000
    c. 2,500
    d. 14,000

23. In 1999 big-breasted blond goddess adult actress Houston made a film called *World's Biggest Gangbang, Part 3*. Afterwards she was a guest on the radio shock jock Howard Stern's show where she said she had sex with how many partners?
    a. 620
    b. 450
    c. 310
    d. 100

24. Erica Jong made this thing famous when she wrote about it in her autobiographical novel, *Fear of Flying*:
    a. The blowjob
    b. Indiscriminate fast sex with a stranger
    c. The mile-high club
    d. Doggie style

25. What was Linda Lovelace's next career path after she was through being the *Deep Throat* girl?
    a. She became a television evangelist.
    b. She became a dog trainer.
    c. She became an antiporn crusader.
    d. She became a stunt car driver.

26. Which popular sportscaster became the object of a tabloid feeding frenzy when he was charged with and arrested on felony charges of forcible sodomy?
    a. Howard Cosell
    b. Don Meredith
    c. Marv Albert
    d. Curt Gowdy

27. This politician died in the arms of his mistress, much to the dismay and embarrassment of his wealthy family. Who were the unlucky couple?
    a. John Lindsay and Bess Myerson
    b. Roy Cohn and Jim Neighbors
    c. Nelson Rockefeller and Megan Marshak
    d. George Romney and Angie Dickinson

28. Who is Heidi Fleiss?
   a. She was a girlfriend of Captain Lou Albano.
   b. She was a prostitute.
   c. She was an actress who underwent a sex change going from he to she.
   d. She was known as the Tinseltown Madam for running a high-priced prostitution ring servicing Hollywood's rich and famous.

Answers to Sexual Personalities

1. a. Casey Donovan, whose real name was Cal Culver, began as a legitimate stage actor and then became a great icon of porn. Often referred to as the gay Robert Redford, this beautiful, golden-haired boy became a legend in gay porn. Culver/ Donovan was a fascinating, hedonistic creature. The combination of his outstanding acting melded with his delicious physique earned him an instant cult following. *Boys in the Sand* was ballyhooed as the groundbreaking catalyst for moving porn actors into the mainstream. A breakthrough film, it featured real actors and a story and a script. But the crossover never happened and Culver/Donovan ultimately became a tragic figure whose imprint on gay culture lingers to this day. *Boys in the Sand* became an albatross around Culver's neck. Casey Donovan he was and Casey Donovan he remains—forever.

2. b. Dutch-born Xaviera Hollander did not invent sex, although millions thought she did. The author of *The Happy Hooker*, published in 1971, was heralded for her humor, her honesty, and her candid approach to sex. Hollander began her long writing career in Australia as a copywriter for J. Walter Thompson. After coming to America, she became secretary to the Dutch consul and, later, the Belgian ambassador. When her

romantic liaison with one or both of these men broke up, she invested $10,000 to buy the client list of a retiring madam to augment her slender secretarial salary. It was the best investment this money-minded Dutch lady could make. So gifted was she at managing girls, customers, and money, that she was heralded (and denounced) as the most influential madam in New York during the late 1960s. While she was penning an advice column for *Penthouse*, Hollander was pursued and persecuted by the Knapp Commission, resulting in her expulsion from the United States. Very much alive and kicking, today she writes about love and food, and lives in Spain, although she returns quite often to her native Holland. In 2002 she authored a sequel memoir entitled *Child No More*.

3. c. A plucky Russian immigrant who graduated from the gritty sweatshops of New York, Polly Adler went on to become the most celebrated madam of her day. As the proprietor and hostess of an opulently decorated string of private clubs in Manhattan, Adler entertained high society, and catered to politicians and mobsters, sometimes simultaneously. Among her closest friends were writers Dorothy Parker and Robert Benchley, two of the most famous members of the Algonquin Round Table. While prostitutes were available to her clients, many of them came just for the company, backgammon, and cards. During Prohibition, Adler was able to get her hands on booze, turning her rooms, as she called them, into speakeasies. For years she dated and protected mob boss Dutch Schultz, who may or may not have been the great love of her life. Adler was constantly being raided by corrupt police whom she had to pay off in bribes. Summoned to appear before the Seabury Commission in the 1930s investigating corrupt cops and judges, Adler wouldn't talk. Although she was permitted to remain in business for a few more years, eventually the police nabbed her and she did a 30-day stint

in jail in 1935. She never returned to the business of prostitution, and took her college degree at the age of fifty. With a ghostwriting collaborator, she authored her autobiography, *A House Is Not a Home*, published in 1951. Her last days were spent in Hollywood where in 1962 she died.

4. d. Austrian psychiatrist Wilhelm Reich was, for many years, the chief associate of Sigmund Freud. After a feud, he broke with Freud, as well as the entire psychoanalytic movement, to pursue his keen interest in biophysics. Forced out of Nazi Germany, Reich arrived in New York City and began teaching at the New School for Social Research. In 1942 he founded the Orgone Institute to promote his theories. His great masterpiece—or Achilles' heel—was his invention of the Orgone Box, a device he claimed would restore energy and increase and measure orgasms. The Food and Drug Administration called it a hoax. A founding father of the as-yet-unnamed sexual revolution, Reich wrote that sexuality was "the center around which revolves the whole of social life as well as the inner life of the individual." His success in captivating the public raised the ire of the U.S. government, which burned all his books and papers and destroyed his Orgone Box. In 1956 he was tried for contempt of court and violation of the Food and Drug Act, and was sentenced to two years in a federal penitentiary where he died.

5. b. Jim Buckley was Al Goldstein's partner when they started the outrageous sex magazine *Screw* in 1969. Buckley was the quiet one as Al Goldstein hogged the show, but Buckley was crying all the way to the bank. The magazine was phenomenally successful with its combination of hooker ads, porn book reviews, and outrageous sexual and political parody. As for Buckley, he morphed into a porn movie producer who, with his brother David, made the 1970s cult classic *Debbie Does Dallas*.

6. d. Mae West, as much a true sexual pioneer as she was an entertaining performer, was one of the first 20th-century women to truly capitalize on the eroticism of her particularly voluptuous anatomy. While other actresses took on roles where their sex appeal was used as a means to an end, West was clear that for her sex *was* the goal. A gifted writer as well as entertainer, her first and most infamous play, *Sex*, was penned in 1926 and West appeared on stage as its star. Almost immediately arrested for obscenity, she was ordered by the judge to serve ten days in jail. "What about my nights?" she responded, spawning one of her famously humorous quotes. West was jailed several times and often criticized for her corrupting influence. The nine films she made during the Depression for Paramount singlehandedly saved that company from bankruptcy. Even dead, West is an icon.

7. b. Julian Eltinge was the most famous female impersonator of all time, carving the way for later impersonators such as Milton Berle and RuPaul. Dubbed "Mr. Lillian Russell," Eltinge was stealing his mama's clothes from the age of ten. As a result of his great flair for dressing up, Eltinge became a vaudeville star who made his debut at the London Palace Theatre in 1906. When he appeared at the Alhambra Theatre in New York in 1907, attired in drop-dead gorgeous gowns, his hair and make-up perfect, the audience was unaware of his gender—he was simply billed "Eltinge"—until he removed his wig after the second act. Eltinge had a brief but successful screen career before returning to what he did best, which was transvestite-loaded vaudeville, writing, casting, and producing sketches for his troupe, the Julian Eltinge Players. The troupe had a hit show in Los Angeles produced by William Morris in 1919. Eltinge was constantly having to prove his masculinity, which sometimes led to fistfights with stagehands, fellow vaudevillians, and even

members of the audience who questioned his sexual preferences. Although many women declared him virile, he never
married, and spent the last years of his life with his mother on
a ranch he bought in California. In 1912 a Broadway theater
was named after him and the Julian Eltinge Theatre on 42nd
Street was a popular destination for tourists and theater addicts
for decades, until the 1980s when redevelopment of the Times
Square area shut it down.

8. b. Master of the macabre Edgar Allen Poe was involved in
numerous scrapes and freaky arrangements involving married
women, a cigar-selling young woman who turned up dead, and
smoldering female poets. Probably one of the more tongue-
wagging episodes in Poe's scandal-pocked life, save his long love
affair with the bottle, was his fevered courtship and subsequent
marriage to his barely pubescent cousin, Virginia Clemm. Eye-
brows shot up again shortly after his marriage when he published *To My Mother*, a poem which appears to be an ode to Mrs.
Maria Clemm, his aunt and mother-in-law. Despite his strange
reputation, Poe was acknowledged to have been a loving husband
to his young cousin. But during their marriage, he became
involved in a twisted love affair with another poet, Frances
Sargent Locke Osgood, and Virginia grew sick and died at the age
of 24. Poe went on to become involved with other women,
including the poets Sarah Ellen Whitman and Susan Archer
Talley. The great love of his life was Elmira Royster, the young
lady who inspired him to write his great poem *Annabel Lee*.

9. c. In 1921, following a lurid three-day party at the St. Fran-
cis Hotel in San Francisco, America's most beloved silent-screen
comedian, Fatty Arbuckle, was vilified in the newspapers for
the death of a young starlet, Virginia Rappe, who reporters said
had been raped and crushed by Arbuckle's enormous weight.

Rank rumors involving a glass bottle in a very inopportune place abounded, and William Randolph Hearst directed his editors to print every one of them, saying the story sold more papers than any event since the sinking of the *Lusitania*. The case resulted in two trials with hung juries until Arbuckle was acquitted in a third trial. His wife stuck by him and was shouted at by angry former fans on the courthouse steps. Arbuckle's career was ruined even though juries found little evidence connecting him to the girl's death. Arbuckle may have been set up by a woman known as Madame Black, Maude Delmont, who provided girls for parties. Fearing reprisals in the form of death by association, Hollywood dropped Arbuckle. He tried getting work as a director under assumed names, but he was finished and died in ignominy and shame in 1933 at the age of 46.

10. a. The Roman emperor Tiberius was one of the first documented pederasts. He built himself a swimming pool and used it as his preferred place to seduce little children. Parents handing their young boys over to influential men to be molested was a common practice in ancient Rome. Plutarch, in fact, wrote a long essay on exactly what kind of person should be the one a dad gives his son to for ritual buggering. Sexual slavery and child prostitution was a flourishing trade, and by law schools were forbidden to stay open past sundown to prevent the students from being molested by their teachers. An entire culture of pederasty was the norm. Suetonius, the chronicler of the private and perverted lives of the Caesars, wrote that under the guise of play, Tiberius instructed children "of the most tender age," kids he called his "little fishes," to swim naked and cavort between his legs as he reclined in his pool/bathtub. Some were so young, they were still being nursed by their mothers. He especially liked toddlers, and played with and sucked their penises. Was he a great Roman emperor, or just a sicko?

11. c. Eva Braun was fresh out of the convent when she was introduced to Adolph Hitler. Instantly smitten, she agreed to follow him to his Alps mountain retreat. In 1936 she moved into his Berghof at Berchtesgaden. Few people, however, including Hitler's political cronies, were aware of her existence. For sixteen years she lived in idle luxury, watching romantic films and tending to her appearance, as millions suffered and died around her. "I live only for your love," she wrote Hitler in a passionate letter. Eva's devotion to her man never flagged, and on the morning of April 29, 1945, a local magistrate married them. A little more than twenty-four hours later, the newlyweds bit into vials of cyanide. Hitler, not wanting to take any chances, also shot himself in the head. The bodies of the star-crossed lovers were carried into the garden by Hitler's inner circle, doused with gasoline, and burned.

12. d. Wayne Lonergan was a handsome, Depression-era, poor youth who met and married the rich, beautiful socialite and brewing-company heiress Patricia Burton. Lonergan was a male gold-digger who swung both ways. After only a few years of marriage, Patricia discovered Wayne was seeing a man, and she couldn't stop taunting him. During an act of oral sex, Patricia bit Lonergan's penis. His reaction was to grab the lamp on a bedside table to beat her to death. He went into hiding for a few days before he was arrested. The bit-off portion of his penis never was found. Lonergan was tried and convicted of murder. Because of the dead woman's social position, the headlines were scalding. Gordon Merrick, one of the first novelists to depict gay life for the masses, told his own fictionalized version of the story in his book *The Good Life*, which offers an intriguing study of homosexual relationships in an era that pre-dated gay social identity. More recently, Dominick Dunne wrote about the case

in his book *Justice*, which includes a chapter on the 1943–44 trial and conviction.

13. a. In 1763 Catherine the Great became the Empress of Russia. One of the most persistent rumors of all time is her sexual fascination with horses. It also happens to be one of the most taboo fascinations, humans coupling with animals. Catherine's marriage to Peter III was a loveless and seemingly sexless marriage—Catherine was a virgin seven years after her wedding night. After her ascension to the throne, she became very public about her sex life. A formidable horsewoman, no doubt she was very fond of horses. But Catherine did not die from being crushed under some horse's great weight during coupling as rumored. Instead she died on the throne, the commode throne—her toilet—probably of a stroke.

14. d. Rasputin was a shadowy and mysterious character. Living in the time of Nicholas and Alexandra, Rasputin was either a gifted miracle worker or an incredible charlatan. After he "saved" a woman after a terrible train accident, a number of influential churchmen called him a holy man, but it seems his great gift lay in his powers of seduction, as he is rumored to have slept with the Empress, her daughters, and Anna Vryubova, the Tsarita's closest friend. Rasputin dragged Alexandra's name through the mud, but women all over Russia swooned for him.

15. b. Bob Crane, the star of the 1960s smash hit *Hogan's Heroes*, had a complicated lifestyle. In love with the newly invented VTR, or video tape recorder, Crane went on wild sex binges recording himself and his party guy-pal, John Carpenter, a sound technician. Both were turned on to the joys of home-made porn. Crane was clubbed to death with his own camera

tripod in a dingy hotel room in 1978, but the murder remains unsolved. Crane's sitcom stardom, his penchant for the orgy scene and the hard-partying Hollywood lifestyle, and his particular obsession with videosex became the subject of Paul Schrader's movie *Auto Focus*.

16. d. Paul Reubens, a native of Peekskill, New York, fashioned himself as a comic character—a quirky, bow-tie-wearing ubernerd man-child. He starred in his wild creation, *Pee Wee's Playhouse*, which ran from 1986 through 1991, turning it into a Saturday morning children's programming classic. Fans of all ages tuned in to watch, but the show abruptly ended when Reubens, wearing a three-day-old beard and no bow tie was arrested in Florida on July 26, 1991 for alleged indecent exposure and masturbation at a porn movie theater in Sarasota. Reubens entered a no-contest plea and was sentenced to 75 hours of community service.

17. d. Nabbed on charges of extortion and tax fraud, porn czar Reuben Sturman was a Cleveland businessman with a knack for making money, particularly from the distribution of porn. Some of the raunchier titles Sturman was associated with include *Dr. Bizarro*, *Between the Cheeks*, *Animal Tapes 1–6*, and *The Nurse Will See You Now*. Charged many times over the years for illegal distribution, Sturman is said to have enjoyed watching juries study his films, and laughing as they passed judgment. His troubles with the government began in 1964, eventually leading up to a massive obscenity case in Las Vegas in 1992 which landed him in jail. Sturman died in 1997 while incarcerated at the age of 73 at a federal prison in Kentucky.

18. a. It seemed like nothing could stand in the way of political golden boy Gary Hart, an openminded politician whose

career was derailed by scandal. Hart's 1988 involvement with model Donna Rice emerged after a photograph was released of her sitting on his very much married presidential candidate's lap on a cruise boat called, most fittingly, *Monkey Business*. The scandal and the photograph effectively ended his run for the White House. Hart dismissed the seriousness of the incident, pointing out that focus should be on real problems such as poverty or war, not on trivia such as who might be sitting on his lap. Twenty years later, the possibility of his being a presidential candidate rose again. Would the public forget or forgive?

19. d. Ivory Snow was the soap flake product manufactured by Procter & Gamble that Marilyn Chambers was selling. Marilyn was only seventeen years old in 1972 when she posed for one of her first modeling jobs, on the Ivory Snow box. A year later all hell broke loose when it was revealed that the slender, willowy model was not a housewifely young mom at all, but a wicked porn star. In 1973 she appeared in *Behind the Green Door*. Procter & Gamble threw a public fit, which helped Chambers' porn career and also sold a lot of laundry detergent. Later it became an in-joke when every film Marilyn appeared in featured a box of Ivory Snow. Brooke Shields was the infant that Marilyn held in the picture that appeared on the soap box.

20. b. Producer Albert Z. Freedman got caught when it came out that America's most popular quiz show, *The Sixty-Four-Thousand-Dollar Question*, was rigged. In 1957, when federal investigators uncovered the corruption beneath the show's glittering façade, Freedman, along with producers Dan Enright and Dick Goodwin—as well as the show's contestants Herbie Stempel and Charles Van Doren—had to take the stand. Freedman's plea for mercy, "It's not like we're hardened criminals here. We're in show business," became famous, although it did not help him

escape an indictment. Freedman fled the country to avoid jail time only to resurface years later in 1965 as one of the money men behind then-unknown Italian photographer and *Penthouse* publisher Bob Guccione. Freedman also appointed himself publisher of *Penthouse*'s digest publications, *Forum* and *Variations*. In the movie "Quiz Show," he was portrayed by the actor Hank Azaria.

21. b. The first black Miss America's image was tarnished when *Penthouse* magazine publisher Bob Guccione ran nude pictures during her 1984 reign. The pictures had been taken years before by the small-time modeling photographer Williams used to do her headshots. Guccione was annoyed at the media fallout, pointing out that she'd signed a release and that he "didn't take his clothes off, she did." The Vanessa Williams issue generated a $14-million profit, the highest in the history of the magazine. Incidentally, that September issue also featured a centerfold of the 15-year-old Traci Lords, who was underage, posing illegally.

22. d. Boaster, liar, or possibly swordmaster nonpareil, John Curtis Holmes, the great "Johnny Wadd," star of countless porn films and featured stud in hundreds of porn-magazine layouts, by his own count had sex with 14,000 women.

23. a. Houston beat Jasmine St. Clair's 1996 record of gang-banging 300 different men by more than twice. Unlike St. Clair, however, Houston made no secret of her contempt for the entire situation and for the porn industry. Not a personal fan of gangbangs or even group sex in particular, Houston told Stern she did it strictly for an undisclosed amount of money.

24. b. Author Erica Jong, whose 1973 novel *Fear of Flying* put her on the map, made fast, indiscriminate sex popular with

her description of something she called "The Zipless Fuck." Jong's fictional character, based loosely on her own id, engages in quickie sex throughout the book, a great deal of it managed without the characters unzipping anything.

25. c. Linda Lovelace, who could never escape her past as the *Deep Throat* girl, became an antiporn crusader. Linda Boreman—her real name—said she had been beaten and coerced into performing in the film by her Svengali-like and abusive husband/manager Chuck Traynor, who she said drugged her and forced her to do the scene at gunpoint. Traynor (who later hooked up with Marilyn Chambers) is reputed to have coerced Linda even before *Deep Throat* into making crude 8-mm films known in the porn industry as "loops," including a much-rumored one of her having sex with a dog. Lovelace made her last film, a softcore porn spoof called *Linda Lovelace for President* in 1974. She disappeared for a time, resurfacing as the author of two tell-all memoirs, *Ordeal* and *Out of Bondage*, recounting her abuse and experiences. As an antiporn crusader she appeared before congressional committees and toured the country with feminists to speak at colleges and universities. Not a proponent of censorship, Boreman billed herself as a "proponent of awareness" about the adult industry. Down on her luck, she posed for a layout in *Leg Show* magazine in 2001. She died in a car accident on April 3, 2002 at the age of 53.

26. c. Marv Albert of NBC eventually pleaded guilty to a reduced charge of assault and battery in a sex-related case brought against him by Vanessa Perhach, his mistress for ten years. Among other complaints, Perhach said Albert bit her. Albert had to resign from his coveted job as the announcer for the Madison Square Garden Network. Before his fall, Albert was a broadcaster for the New York Knicks, Rangers, and Giants

who'd worked five NBA Finals, an NBA All-Star Game, the 1992 Summer Olympics in Barcelona, and the 1994 Basketball World Championships. Quickly forgiven by the general public, Albert was rehired by the MSG and Turner networks in 1998, and was back at NBC in 1999.

27. c. Powerful and wealthy Nelson Rockefeller was a former governor of New York as well as Gerald Ford's veep. To the dismay of his family and delight of the tabloids, the famously randy Rockefeller expired of a sudden heart attack while with his mistress, a former White House staff member, Megan Marshak. Rockefeller died in the very same townhouse he had bought for Marshak's use and left her in his will. Reporters said the body had been moved to another room and placed in a sitting-up position by the time the police arrived. Although it was widely speculated that Rockefeller died in Marshak's bed, she told the press they were working late on an art book project. After Rockefeller's death, Marshak, then 27, was hired to write news for WCBS-TV.

28. d. Heidi Fleiss was born in Los Angeles in 1965. The daughter of a Hollywood pediatrician, Fleiss ran a string of high-class call girls who were said to charge $1500 a night for their services. When she was nabbed in 1995 as part of an undercover sting operation, it turned out that Charlie Sheen was the only celebrity listed in her "black book." Fleiss served three years in jail for tax evasion and money laundering. A movie, *Heidi Fleiss: Hollywood Madam*, was released in the United Kingdom in 1995.

The Kama Sutra

THE *KAMA SUTRA*, often referred to as the Bible of sex, is a very old book, a true relic and antique. While many have heard of it, not so many have read it, and even less understand what a refined and informative (and thrilling!) document it is. Exhaustively examined, studied, disclaimed, revered, and rejected, it has been considered pornography in some cultures. But the *Kama Sutra* is a very valuable resource. In no other book can one find so much and so varied information dedicated totally to sex. The *Kama Sutra* is very old but very special. To test your ultimate sexual knowledge, see how much you know about this treasure trove of sexual lore!

1. The *Kama Sutra* is said to have been originally written by an Indian gentleman by the family name of Vatsyayana. The present translation, postdating ones done centuries ago by Indian scholars, was written by which two Englishmen?
   a. D. H. Lawrence and Percy Bysshe Shelley
   b. Virginia Woolf and George Eliot
   c. Sir Richard Burton and F. F. Arbuthnot
   d. Oscar Wilde and The Marquis of Queensbury

2. The English versions of the *Kama Sutra* are translated from what language?
   a. Sanskrit
   b. Arabic
   c. Hebrew
   d. Urdu

3. The underlying Hindu perspective on sex is that sex is:
   a. Statutory
   b. Sinful
   c. Sacramental
   d. Sentimental

4. The original *Kama Sutra* appears to have been composed between which centuries?
   a. The second and sixth centuries A.D.
   b. The first and fourth centuries A.D.
   c. The fifth and sixth centuries A.D.
   d. Before Christ

5. The present-day version of the *Kama Sutra* contains _____ chapters and is divided into _____ sections.
   a. 100 chapters and 25 sections
   b. 101 chapters and 16 sections
   c. 150 chapters and 7 sections
   d. 25 chapters and 100 sections

6. Part II of the *Kama Sutra* is focused on sex acts which involve:
   a. Oral sex
   b. Courtesans and women of pleasure
   c. A woman other than one's wife
   d. Kissing, embracing, and marking one's partner with one's nails

7. The word "lingam" means:
   a. Anus
   b. Throat
   c. Penis
   d. Navel

8. When a man presses the middle part of the woman's body against his own and kisses or lightly scratches her torso, this is called:
   a. Worshipping the deity
   b. The precepts of the Holy Writ
   c. The mark of the tiger's nail
   d. The embrace of the jaghana

9. A kiss where one lover's tongue connects with the other's tongue, teeth, or roof of the mouth, is called:
   a. Peacock kiss
   b. Fighting of the tongue
   c. The kiss that awakens
   d. The kiss that kindles love

10. Acceptable locations on the body to scratch your partner's flesh are:
    a. The insides of the thighs and the buttocks
    b. The nape of the neck
    c. The armpit, the throat, the breasts, the lips, the belly, and thighs
    d. Behind the knees and in the crook of the elbow

11. When five marks of the nails are made near the nipple of the breast, this is called:
    a. Jump of the hare
    b. Leap of the fox
    c. The circle of wonder
    d. The half moon

12. When a small portion of the skin is bitten using all the teeth, this is called:
   a. A line
   b. The peacock's foot
   c. Token of remembrance
   d. The point

13. When a woman raises her thighs and holds them far apart while she is being penetrated, this is called:
   a. The opening of the cave
   b. The yawning position
   c. The invitation to Heaven
   d. Vatsayana's delight

14. When a woman places her head lower than her midsection during copulation, this position is known as:
   a. The belly of the beast
   b. The dog position
   c. The widely opened position
   d. The temple position

15. In the *Kama Sutra*, a woman's vagina is referred to as:
   a. Her treasure
   b. Her linga
   c. Her yoni
   d. Her riches

16. When a woman holds a man captive inside her body using the muscles of her vagina, this is called:
   a. The cat's position
   b. The mare's position
   c. The spider position
   d. The elephant position

17. According to the *Kama Sutra*, when a man lies on his left side, what side should the woman always lie on?
    a. Her right side
    b. Her left side
    c. They should keep turning until they're the most comfortable
    d. She should lie on her stomach

18. When a woman rests her legs on top of her lover's shoulders and alternately scissors her legs this is called:
    a. The splitting of the bamboo
    b. The shifting of the tides
    c. The coming of the storm
    d. The scissors

19. In the *Kama Sutra*, the phrase "sporting of a sparrow," means:
    a. To have sex with more than one person within a 24-hour period
    b. To interrupt intercourse in order to eat or drink
    c. To have sex with a man with an exceptionally small penis
    d. To have sex for hours without stopping

20. In the *Kama Sutra*, when only the inner lips of the vagina experience friction by the penis, this is known as:
    a. The breathing of the weasel
    b. The blow of the boar
    c. The bouncing of the baboon
    d. The breeching of the bear

21. Who should never assume the female superior—woman on top—position according to the *Kama Sutra*:
    a. A woman who has just eaten dinner
    b. A woman with weak legs
    c. A woman who has recently lost her father, a woman who came to the marriage without a dowry, or an old woman
    d. A woman having her period, a woman who's recently given birth, or a fat woman

22. In the *Kama Sutra*, a man who enjoys the pleasures of two women at the same time is said to be:
    a. Engaging in the congress of the goats
    b. Engaging in the congress of a herd of cows
    c. A very rich man
    d. A glutton

23. To what other common human activity does the *Kama Sutra* liken sex?
    a. Eating
    b. Quarreling
    c. Hunting
    d. Going to market

24. An inexperienced young woman to whom one is making love should be first kissed on:
    a. The lips
    b. The throat
    c. The breasts
    d. The arms

25. The erotic act of a man using his penis to strike or slap a woman's vagina is called:
    a. Giving it a blow
    b. Smacking
    c. Tapping
    d. Snapping

26. If a man is exhausted and can't maintain his erection, but his woman wants to keep going, what should he do to satisfy his woman?
    a. Lick her all over
    b. Offer to give her double pleasure on the morrow
    c. Give her a long backrub
    d. Rub her yoni with his hands and fingers

Answers to The Kama Sutra

1. c. Burton and Arbuthnot, two friends in Victorian England, founded the Kama Shastra Society as an excuse to study Hindu erotic literature. Arbuthnot was a retired Indian civil servant and Burton had served as an ensign in the Indian army. Aided by Persian tutors, Burton began his study of Indian languages as a very young man, an interest he maintained throughout his lifetime. Burton was a writer who published throughout his life. The *Kama Sutra* is absolutely not pornography; in fact many esteemed social historians and scholars believe the text of the *Kama Sutra* has had a profound influence on the modern understanding of Indian art and culture for its connection between sexuality and meaningful life.

2. a. The *Kama Sutra* was originally written in Sanskrit, the ancient classical language of India and of Hinduism.

3. c. The Hindu view of sex fundamentally differs from the views of many other cultures. Sex is considered not to be merely normal and necessary, but a sacrament. The religious symbolism of the Hindus focuses on the union of matter and energy in the form of deities said to be responsible for the creation of the world. The symbol of Shiva is the lingam, or phallus, while the symbol of Shakti is the yoni, or vagina. In the earliest literature of the Hindus, the sex act is compared to a sacred sacrifice.

4. b. The *Kama Sutra* is believed to have been written by a man called Mallanaga who lived between the first and the fourth centuries A.D. He was a member of the Vatsyayana family.

5. c. Burton and Arbuthnot chose to reorganize the original thousand chapters into 150 chapters under the following heads or parts: General Topics, Embraces, The Union of Males and Females, Attitudes and Congress with One's Wife, Attitudes and Congress with Wives of Others, Courtesans, Eunuchs, The Art of Seduction, and tonic medicines meant to enhance sexual pleasure.

6. d. In the section on sexual union, part four is entitled, "On Pressing or Marking with the Nails." Proper scratching and marking techniques are outlined in detail, enumerating the eight kinds of marks which may be produced on the lover's body, including but not limited to the half moon, circle, line, peacock's foot, and the leaf of a blue lotus, which each refer to a specific kind of mark. Places where the nail marks may be left are also detailed, as are the size of the nails and their condition.

7. c. In the *Kama Sutra*, the penis or male sexual organ is always referred to as the lingam.

8. d. The embrace of the jaghana basically boils down to the man rubbing, kissing, caressing, biting, scratching—doing anything but penetrating the woman's rectum or vagina. The territory of the jaghana is everything in between the breastbone to pubic bone. Frottage and dry humping count as embraces of the jaghana, too.

9. b. Fighting of the tongue is the correct answer. Kissing is parsed down to the finest minutiae in the *Kama Sutra*. What Westerners call a "french kiss" is given this more dramatic and fanciful name in the translation from the Sanskrit.

10. c. When lovemaking becomes very intense, the *Kama Sutra* allows for leaving marks on the body of the beloved on specific occasions, such as just before one is setting out on a journey, or returning from a journey or when angry lovers have been reconciled. Leaving light scratch marks on the body with the nails is considered perfectly appropriate behavior when lovers are very passionate.

11. a. The origins of this phrase are unclear, but the name "jump of the hare," is both poetic and provocative. There are no less than eleven descriptions given in this section of the *Kama Sutra* for scratching and leaving a mark on someone, or what is known to modern Western peoples as "rough sex." Marking someone is a way of staking a claim; some of these markings require particular skill to correctly execute, and courtesans of the time were well acquainted with a variety of special nail-effects.

12. d. Eight different kinds of biting are described in the *Kama Sutra*, from a simple reddening of the skin to more significant wounding. Women of different regions of India are described in the book for their fondness or rejection of different degrees of

biting and where they prefer to be bitten. The book makes clear that a woman who has been bitten by a man during an act of passion should bite back with double force.

13. b. The *Kama Sutra* describes three positions of so-called "high congress," which are meant to widen a less-experienced woman's vulva for the male's most promising access. These ways of lying down are described as the widely opened position, where the woman is on her hands and knees; the yawning position, where the woman is flat on her back with her legs spread wide open; and the position known as "The Wife of Indra," where the woman lies on her back with her knees drawn to her chest. The yawning position is one that requires no special lubricants, as entrance should be accomplished easily and the position requires no special expertise from the woman. The Wife of Indra is said to be good for a man with a smaller penis as deeper penetration can more easily be achieved.

14. c. The widely opened position can be described in modern English vernacular as "rear entry," or "doggy style." The *Kama Sutra* suggests that the man use some unguent, such as saliva, to facilitate penetration, although it is assumed that once he's got his lingam in, the woman's yoni will be wide open.

15. c. Yoni is the symbol of the deity Shakti. In the Hindu world of belief, Shiva and Shakti are said to be the deities responsible for the creation of the world.

16. b. Considered to be a form of "the lowest congress," along with the clasping position, the pressing position, and the twining position, the mare's position is designed to make a woman's vagina (or yoni) seem smaller. Obviously, a smaller, tighter yoni is more pleasurable for the man. These low-congress positions

are favored for use with women who have had a good deal of sexual experience or who have had several children. When they know they will be engaging in lower congress sex, women are also advised to make use of special so-called medicinal mixtures to facilitate a quickened female orgasm. The mare's position is said to be mastered by great practice only. The people of India's southern regions also refer to anal sex as lower congress.

17. a. The clasping position requires the lovers to either be supine or on their sides. The book dictates that in the side position the male should invariably lie on his left side and the woman on her right. This rule is to be observed in lying down with all kinds of women.

18. a. The origins of this intriguing expression are unclear, even if the position description isn't!

19. d. The characteristics of various animals are used to describe various kinds of sex. Do sparrows have sex for hours without stopping? Apparently the Hindu people believe it to be so!

20. b. The manner in which sex organs are brought together is specifically defined and delineated in the *Kama Sutra*, where every degree of intimacy is spelled out and personified. The "blow of the boar" is a form of foreplay, something that happens before real penetration is achieved. It's a teasing act in which the penis merely rubs or tickles the outer and possibly inner labia, meant to increase anticipation for the serious intercourse that is about to begin.

21. d. While the *Kama Sutra* does not spell out why a menstruating woman, a new mother, or an overweight woman should

decline to assume the female superior pose, these prohibitions were rock-solid rules that lovers adhered to.

22. b. While it's a safe bet that very few women care to be referred to as cows, the image of a bullish man cavorting with several docile women who patiently wait their turn for his sexual attention does bring to mind the bold bull in the company of his lowing bovine harem.

23. b. The *Kama Sutra* compares sexual intercourse to a quarrel because of the contrariness of love and the tendency for lovers to have disputes. In this context, it is acceptable for lovers to strike each other's bodies in the course of passion, the way they might strike someone else in a fight.

24. c. In the detailed sections on marriage and the proper breaking in of a young and virginal wife, the *Kama Sutra* advises that husbands can create confidence in a young girl by not frightening her or scaring her away from sex. While kissing the breasts before the lips strikes modern readers as odd, it must be remembered that the *Kama Sutra* was written in a time when women did not ordinarily cover up their breasts.

25. a. The practice of slapping the penis against the vagina is something commonly seen in modern porn films, but smacking, striking, or otherwise drumming the penis against the outer lips of the vagina is an ancient form of foreplay widely practiced by the East Indian culture. In the *Kama Sutra* it is called "giving it a blow," the "blow" meaning "to strike" as opposed to its Western meaning in "blow job," an oral sexual act.

26. d. According to the *Kama Sutra*, a woman who hasn't had her orgasm may insist her partner finish her off with his hand—even if she has to resort to kicking and biting him.

Interpreting Your Ultimate Score

CONGRATULATIONS! You have completed the test! Now it's time to tally your score to determine your sexual intelligence quotient. Remember: whatever your score turns out to be, always know that when it comes to further educating yourself about sex, the journey is very much part of the destination.

0–1300 points: Libidiot

What you don't know about sex could fill a book! This very one, in fact! You might feel discouraged by your final tally, and if you're taking the quiz with friends they might be giving you a bit of a ribbing! They might raise embarrassing questions about your copulation habits. You might be concerned, and perhaps you should be. Although your score does reflect your sheltered lifestyle and relative innocence, your lack of knowledge about certain aspects of sex could be a hindrance to your personal life. But don't despair. You've got the rest of your life to acquire a solid foundation of knowledge about sex—starting right here. The rewards for such knowledge are very rich indeed. Start by searching out sexier reading matter (the classics are a good place to begin), watching more teen flicks and foreign movies, and expanding your personal sexual repertoire. There's a lot more to life than the missionary position!

1310–2600 points: Middlesexer

You are wonderfully in the middle, caught betwixt and between being a sexual dummy and a sexual genius. This is probably one of the best places in the world to be and you're probably a very happy person, sexually speaking, because you know more than enough to get by, but not so much that you're in danger of being branded as obsessive. You know enough about sex to stay out of trouble, and more than enough to get by! Being caught in the middle (especially if it's in the middle of a person sandwich, sometimes known as a threesome—but you already knew that) is a very fine position. Be comfortable where you are, but don't be afraid to learn things. Speaking of positions, sometimes it's good to be on the bottom—and sometimes it's good to be on top!

2610–3940 points: Sexpert

You are something of a marvel, or you're just marvelous. It's a wonder your friends and lovers can keep up with you, you know so much! Obviously, you have spent a good deal of your life thinking about sex, studying it, reading up on it, analyzing it, scrutinizing it, and with any luck, doing it—or getting done by somebody else! While you are basking in your spectacular grasp of this very wide and tricky subject, try to be a little humble; there are a few downsides to knowing so much about sex, although none leap to mind right at this very moment! Your high score proves beyond a shadow of a doubt that you are a true "sexpert." Congratulations! Now get naked, get out the lube and the sex toys and your stash of secret aphrodisiacs, and celebrate! Hopefully with a real person and not a blow-up doll!

References

I⊤ was no simple task coming up with the number and breadth of questions, not to mention the answers, for a quiz like *What's Your Sexual IQ?* While I thought I already knew a lot, I still had to read a pile of books and consult several websites and talk to oodles of people to compile all the necessary information. Here are the important primary sources used to write this book:

Ashe, Penelope. *Naked Came the Stranger*. New York: Lyle Stuart, 1969.

Blakely, Ann, and Julia Moore. *The Other Rules*. New York: Masquerade, 1998.

Bronson, Fred. *The Billboard Book of Number One Hits*. New York: Billboard Publications, 1988.

Burton, Sir Richard, and F. F. Arbuthnot. *The Kama Sutra of Vatsayana*. New York: Berkeley, 1984.

Cleland, John. *Memoirs of a Woman of Pleasure*. New York: Oxford University Press, reprinted 1986.

Edgerton, Jane E. *The American Psychiatric Glossary, Seventh Edition*. Washington, D.C.: American Psychiatric Press, 1994.

Ernst, Morris L., and David Loth. *American Sexual Behavior and the Kinsey Report*. New York: Bantam, 1948.

Ford, Luke. *The History of X*. New York: Prometheus, 1999.

Harris, Frank. *My Life and Loves*. New York: Grove Press, 1963.

Holliday, Jim. *Only the Best*. n.p. (Calif.): Cal Vista, 1986.

Joyce, James. *Ulysses*. New York: Random House, 1961.

Manson, Marilyn, with Neil Strauss. *The Long Hard Road out of Hell*. New York: Regan Books/HarperCollins, 1999.

McNeill, William H. *Plagues and Peoples*. New York: Anchor, 1976.

Perry, Hamilton Darby. *A Chair for Wayne Lonergan*. New York: Macmillan, 1972.

Réage, Pauline. *The Story of O*. New York: Olympia, 1954.

Roth, Phillip. *Portnoy's Complaint*. New York: Harper Collins, 1969.

Simons, G. L. *The Illustrated Book of Sex Records*. New York: Putnam, 1983.

Spears, Richard A. *Slang and Euphemism*. New York: Jonathan David, 1981.

Taomino, Tristan. *The Ultimate Guide to Anal Sex for Women*. San Francisco: Cleis, 1998.

Tisserand, Maggie. *Essence of Love*. New York: HarperCollins, 1993.

Updike, John. *Couples*. New York: Knopf, 1968.

About the Author

EVE MARX, M.A., is a bona fide Sexpert. A graduate of Columbia University Teacher's College, Marx was an editor of *Penthouse Forum* and *Swank* magazines. Under various pseudonyms, she was an associate editor at *High Society* and *Celebrity Skin* magazines, and wrote quizzes and fiction and feature stories for *Velvet*, *Oui, Oui Letters*, and many other adult publications. She was a regular contributor to *Screw* magazine and a producer for the *Penthouse Phone Sex Tapes*. For many years, under her pseudonym Mary Arno, she reviewed adult films for AVN and Swank Video World. Today she is a newspaper columnist and lifestyle and real-estate writer for *The Bedford Record Review*, *The Westchester County Times*, *The Fairfield County Times*, *The Pet Gazette*, and other regional publications. She is the author of *View from the Porch: Tales from the Anti-Hamptons* and two sex how-to books, *Passion* and *10 Nights of Passion*. Under her pseudonym Ava De Hilliard she is the author of *Erotica: Three Tales of Lust and Passion*. She lives in New York with her family.